Singing the Faith

SERMON HYMNS FOR EVERY SUNDAY

❧✳❧

by

Georg Retzlaff

authorHOUSE®

AuthorHouse™
1663 Liberty Drive
Bloomington, IN 47403
www.authorhouse.com
Phone: 1-800-839-8640

Published by AuthorHouse 2/24/2012

ISBN: 978-1-4685-5306-2 (e)
ISBN: 978-1-4685-5307-9 (sc)

Library of Congress Control Number: 2012903081

*Any people depicted in stock imagery provided by Thinkstock are models,
and such images are being used for illustrative purposes only.
Certain stock imagery © Thinkstock.*

This book is printed on acid-free paper.

*Because of the dynamic nature of the Internet, any web addresses or links contained in this book may have changed
since publication and may no longer be valid. The views expressed in this work are solely those of the author and do
not necessarily reflect the views of the publisher, and the publisher hereby disclaims any responsibility for them.*

Foreword

Cantare est bis orare: St. Augustine was right in his emphasis on singing as a way of praying twice, by adding another dimension to the merely verbal communication as we delve into the realm of emotion and communality. What is even more important is the fact that our understanding of Jesus and His words is rarely, if ever, informed by doctrinal discourse but rather by the hymns we sing. Every Sunday a portion of the gospel is read in church. It is (or should be) preached on, and the choirmaster's Handbook suggests a hymn which supposedly summarizes or encapsulates that message.

After forty years in the pulpit I could not help but sometimes decry the choices given to us. The "official" hymns too often undercut a radical and modern understanding of the gospel by dragging people back into a childlike simplicity and making them toe a musical "party line". I sometimes found myself and my sermons vitiated by lyrics which seemed to contradict what I thought the gospel was all about.

It is for this reason that I found it helpful to write (and compose) hymns which bear out the plain truth of the words of Jesus as I understand them. This book is for those who look for a synthesis between theology and hymnody, who struggle with relevance, with ways to make doctrine singable. This adds a third dimension to the quote by St. Augustine: singing is not just praying but also confessing and proclaiming. Martin Luther knew that Protestant doctrine would not gain a foothold in the population unless it was sung: with lyrics simple, sweet, and true, with melodies either known or attractively new.

This volume contains hymns for every Sunday (of Year A, Revised Common Lectionary) with lyrics set to new tunes, but also using traditional ones found in the Anglican tradition [to which I have added a reference, be it to the Hymnal of the Protestant Episcopal Church (HPEC 1940 or 1982), or to the English

Hymnal (EH 1933), followed by the respective hymn number]. Quite a number of melodies comes from the German folk tradition, long a source of hymnody but also largely ignored in its wealth of musical expression and variety.

I have been blessed with my wife Joy who not only edited my poetry and offered much needed critical advice but who also wrote one of the hymns herself. I also wish to thank Dr. John Lee for allowing me to publish his original tune In My Father's House.

Soli Deo Gloria: may this humble work bless someone somewhere and stir up in them the burning desire to sing their faith into the world.

Epiphany 2012

Georg Retzlaff

Advent I

Matthew 24:36-44

Jesus said to the disciples, "But about that day and hour no one knows, neither the angels of heaven, nor the Son, but only the Father. For as the days of Noah were, so will be the coming of the Son of Man. For as in those days before the flood they were eating and drinking, marrying and giving in marriage, until the day Noah entered the ark, and they knew nothing until the flood came and swept them all away, so too will be the coming of the Son of Man. Then two will be in the field; one will be taken and one will be left. Two women will be grinding meal together; one will be taken and one will be left. Keep awake therefore, for you do not know on what day your Lord is coming. But understand this: if the owner of the house had known in what part of the night the thief was coming, he would have stayed awake and would not have let his house be broken into. Therefore you also must be ready, for the Son of Man is coming at an unexpected hour."

Georg Retzlaff

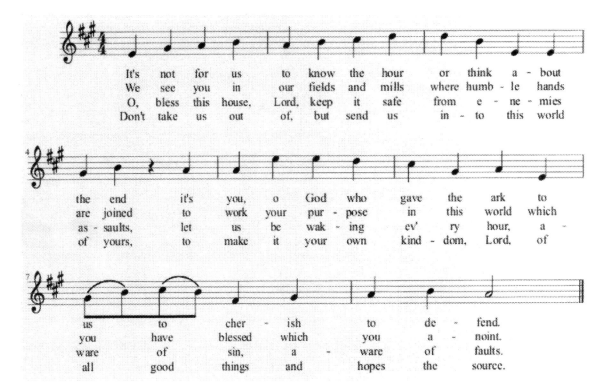

Words: Georg Retzlaff (b. 1946)
Music: *Lillian*, Georg Retzlaff (b. 1946)

86 88

Advent II

Matthew 3:1-12

In those days John the Baptist appeared in the wilderness of Judea, proclaiming, "Repent, for the kingdom of heaven has come near." This is the one of whom the prophet Isaiah spoke when he said, "The voice of one crying out in the wilderness: `Prepare the way of the Lord, make his paths straight.'"Now John wore clothing of camel's hair with a leather belt around his waist, and his food was locusts and wild honey. Then the people of Jerusalem and all Judea were going out to him, and all the region along the Jordan, and they were baptized by him in the river Jordan, confessing their sins.But when he saw many Pharisees and Sadducees coming for baptism, he said to them, "You brood of vipers! Who warned you to flee from the wrath to come? Bear fruit worthy of repentance. Do not presume to say to yourselves, `We have Abraham as our ancestor'; for I tell you, God is able from these stones to raise up children to Abraham. Even now the ax is lying at the root of the trees; every tree therefore that does not bear good fruit is cut down and thrown into the fire. "I baptize you with water for repentance, but one who is more powerful than I is coming after me; I am not worthy to carry his sandals. He will baptize you with the Holy Spirit and fire. His winnowing fork is in his hand, and he will clear his threshing floor and will gather his wheat into the granary; but the chaff he will burn with unquenchable fire."

Georg Retzlaff

From   wa - ter   we   have   come,   of   wa - ter   we   are
By   God's   own   grace   we   see   the   end   of   threat   and
We   who   are   bap - tized   sing   this   song   to   Him   who

made,   in   it   we   are   re - freshed,   re - born,   It
wrath.   We   can,   be   yond   the   dark - ened   sky,   be
came   with   Ho   ly   Spi - rit   and   with   fire   to

takes   a - way   our   sin - ful   Selves,   re - stores   hu - ma - ni -
neath   the   laws   of   right   and   wrong,   the   new - ness   of   God's
move   our   minds   from   sin   and   death   to   deep   and   hea - ven -

ty   for - lorn.
will   de - scry.
ly   de - sire.

Words: Georg Retzlaff (b. 1946)
Music: *Kansas*, Georg Retzlaff (b. 1946)

66 888

Advent III

Matthew 11:2-11

When John heard in prison what the Messiah was doing, he sent word by his disciples and said to him, "Are you the one who is to come, or are we to wait for another?" Jesus answered them, "Go and tell John what you hear and see: the blind receive their sight, the lame walk, the lepers are cleansed, the deaf hear, the dead are raised, and the poor have good news brought to them. And blessed is anyone who takes no offense at me." As they went away, Jesus began to speak to the crowds about John: "What did you go out into the wilderness to look at? A reed shaken by the wind? What then did you go out to see? Someone dressed in soft robes? Look, those who wear soft robes are in royal palaces. What then did you go out to see? A prophet? Yes, I tell you, and more than a prophet. This is the one about whom it is written, 'See, I am sending my messenger ahead of you, who will prepare your way before you.' Truly I tell you, among those born of women no one has arisen greater than John the Baptist; yet the least in the kingdom of heaven is greater than he."

Georg Retzlaff

The wait is o'er, the hour is now when Christ - ians
Our God does speak where' er He will to sa - ges
A mid con - fus - ion and dis - may your peop - le

must de - cide: Whom will I fol - low? It's not the world's speak -
far and near. Whom will I fol - low? Not proph - et of dooms -
seek the Truth. Whom will they fol - low? Be ware of the wolves

ers, nor one of its preach - ers, but Je - sus a - lone.
day, pur - vey - ors of hear - say, but Je - sus a - lone.
and their sheep's clothes! And then stand on Je - sus a - lone.

Words: Georg Retzlaff (b. 1946)
Music: *Heiligkreuz*, Georg Retzlaff (b. 1946)

865 665

Advent IV

Matthew 1:18-25

Now the birth of Jesus the Messiah took place in this way. When his mother Mary had been engaged to Joseph, but before they lived together, she was found to be with child from the Holy Spirit. Her husband Joseph, being a righteous man and unwilling to expose her to public disgrace, planned to dismiss her quietly. But just when he had resolved to do this, an angel of the Lord appeared to him in a dream and said, "Joseph, son of David, do not be afraid to take Mary as your wife, for the child conceived in her is from the Holy Spirit. She will bear a son, and you are to name him Jesus, for he will save his people from their sins." All this took place to fulfill what had been spoken by the Lord through the prophet: "Look, the virgin shall conceive and bear a son, and they shall name him Emmanuel," which means, "God is with us." When Joseph awoke from sleep, he did as the angel of the Lord commanded him; he took her as his wife, but had no marital relations with her until she had borne a son; and he named him Jesus.

Georg Retzlaff

We praise you, God, for Ma - ry, the bles - sed mot - her of our
We praise you, God, for Jo - seph, the Spi - rit dream - er, gent - le
We praise you, God, for Je - sus, Em - man - u - el, our ve - ry
We praise you, God Al - migh - ty, who chose to be with us al -

Lord, who car - ried her child with ten - der - ness mild and
man, who fos - tered the son, and gave him a home, and
joy who grew to be bold to ques - tion our old re -
ways, who gave us the Word, which we, when we heard, will

faith as her on - ly re - ward.
did what so few fath - ers can.
li - gion, and doubt to de - stroy.
glad - ly pro - fess all our days.

Words: Georg Retzlaff (b. 1946)
Music: *Boswell*, Georg Retzlaff (b. 1946)

78 558

Christmas Day II

Luke 2:(1-7) 8-20

[In those days a decree went out from Emperor Augustus that all the world should be registered. This was the first registration and was taken while Quirinius was governor of Syria. All went to their own towns to be registered. Joseph also went from the town of Nazareth in Galilee to Judea, to the city of David called Bethlehem, because he was descended from the house and family of David. He went to be registered with Mary, to whom he was engaged and who was expecting a child. While they were there, the time came for her to deliver her child. And she gave birth to her firstborn son and wrapped him in bands of cloth, and laid him in a manger, because there was no place for them in the inn.] In that region there were shepherds living in the fields, keeping watch over their flock by night. Then an angel of the Lord stood before them, and the glory of the Lord shone around them, and they were terrified. But the angel said to them, "Do not be afraid; for see-- I am bringing you good news of great joy for all the people: to you is born this day in the city of David a Savior, who is the Messiah, the Lord. This will be a sign for you: you will find a child wrapped in bands of cloth and lying in a manger." And suddenly there was with the angel a multitude of the heavenly host, praising God and saying,

"Glory to God in the highest heaven,
     and on earth peace among those whom he favors!"

When the angels had left them and gone into heaven, the shepherds said to one another, "Let us go now to Bethlehem and see this thing that has taken place, which the Lord has made known to us." So they went with haste and found Mary and Joseph, and the child lying in the manger. When they saw this, they made known what had been told them about this child; and all who heard it were amazed at what the shepherds told them. But Mary treasured all these words and pondered them in her heart. The shepherds returned, glorifying and praising God for all they had heard and seen, as it had been told them.

Georg Retzlaff

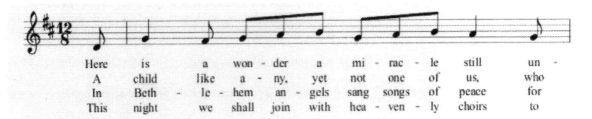

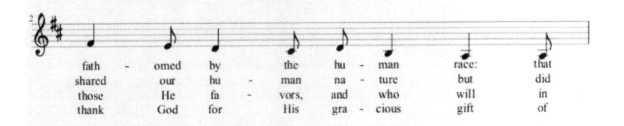

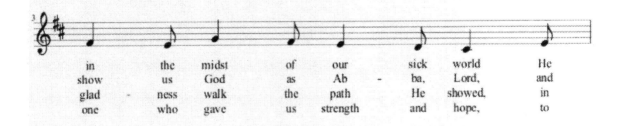

Words: Georg Retzlaff (b. 1946)
Music: *Beverly*, Georg Retzlaff (b. 1946)

10 888

Christmas Day III

John 1:1-14

In the beginning was the Word, and the Word was with God, and the Word was God. He was in the beginning with God. All things came into being through him, and without him not one thing came into being. What has come into being in him was life, and the life was the light of all people. The light shines in the darkness, and the darkness did not overcome it. There was a man sent from God, whose name was John. He came as a witness to testify to the light, so that all might believe through him. He himself was not the light, but he came to testify to the light. The true light, which enlightens everyone, was coming into the world. He was in the world, and the world came into being through him; yet the world did not know him. He came to what was his own, and his own people did not accept him. But to all who received him, who believed in his name, he gave power to become children of God, who were born, not of blood or of the will of the flesh or of the will of man, but of God. And the Word became flesh and lived among us, and we have seen his glory, the glory as of a father's only son, full of grace and truth.

Georg Retzlaff

The Word be-came flesh, when first it was spo - ken,
The Word took on form, be - yond sound and gram - mar,
The Word still pro-claimed, from lec - tern and pul - pit,
The Word wants to dwell in hearts of be - lie - vers

when light did ap - pear the world to re - fresh.
in Him who spoke truth and lived in the storm.
will reach all the hearts of those who are maimed.
who live it and dare to share and to tell.

the world to re - fresh.
and lived in the storm.
of those who are maimed.
to share and to tell.

Words: Georg Retzlaff (b. 1946)
Music: *First Street*, Georg Retzlaff (b. 1946)

5 6 5 5

First Sunday after Christmas

John 1:1-18

In the beginning was the Word, and the Word was with God, and the Word was God. He was in the beginning with God. All things came into being through him, and without him not one thing came into being. What has come into being in him was life, and the life was the light of all people. The light shines in the darkness, and the darkness did not overcome it. There was a man sent from God, whose name was John. He came as a witness to testify to the light, so that all might believe through him. He himself was not the light, but he came to testify to the light. The true light, which enlightens everyone, was coming into the world. He was in the world, and the world came into being through him; yet the world did not know him. He came to what was his own, and his own people did not accept him. But to all who received him, who believed in his name, he gave power to become children of God, who were born, not of blood or of the will of the flesh or of the will of man, but of God. And the Word became flesh and lived among us, and we have seen his glory, the glory as of a father's only son, full of grace and truth. (John testified to him and cried out, "This was he of whom I said, 'He who comes after me ranks ahead of me because he was before me.'") From his fullness we have all received, grace upon grace. The law indeed was given through Moses; grace and truth came through Jesus Christ. No one has ever seen God. It is God the only Son, who is close to the Father's heart, who has made him known.

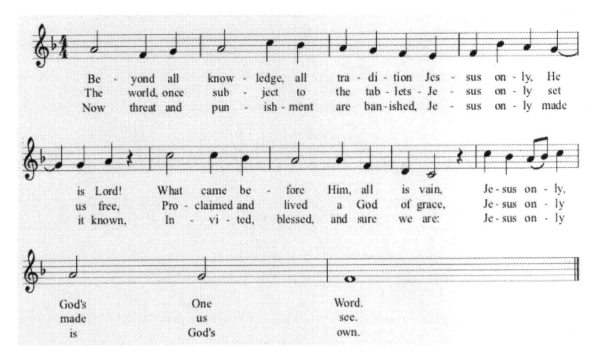

Be - yond all know - ledge, all tra - di - tion Jes - sus on - ly, He
The world, once sub - ject to the tab - lets - Je - sus on - ly set
Now threat and pun - ish - ment are ban - ished, Je - sus on - ly made

is Lord! What came be - fore Him, all is vain, Je - sus on - ly,
us free, Pro - claimed and lived a God of grace, Je - sus on - ly
it known, In - vi - ted, blessed, and sure we are: Je - sus on - ly

God's One Word.
made us see.
is God's own.

Words: Georg Retzlaff (b. 1946)
Music: *Suacoco*, Georg Retzlaff (b. 1946)

9 7 8 7

Second Sunday after Christmas

Matthew 2:13-15,19-23

Now after the wise men had left, an angel of the Lord appeared to Joseph in a dream and said, "Get up, take the child and his mother, and flee to Egypt, and remain there until I tell you; for Herod is about to search for the child, to destroy him." Then Joseph got up, took the child and his mother by night, and went to Egypt, and remained there until the death of Herod. This was to fulfill what had been spoken by the Lord through the prophet, "Out of Egypt I have called my son."When Herod died, an angel of the Lord suddenly appeared in a dream to Joseph in Egypt and said, "Get up, take the child and his mother, and go to the land of Israel, for those who were seeking the child's life are dead." Then Joseph got up, took the child and his mother, and went to the land of Israel. But when he heard that Archelaus was ruling over Judea in place of his father Herod, he was afraid to go there. And after being warned in a dream, he went away to the district of Galilee. There he made his home in a town called Nazareth, so that what had been spoken through the prophets might be fulfilled, "He will be called a Nazorean."

Words: Georg Retzlaff (b. 1946)
Music: *St. Mark's*, Georg Retzlaff (b. 1946)

76 74 46

The Epiphany

Mt 2:1-12

Now when Jesus was born in Bethlehem of Judea in the days of Herod the king, behold, wise men from the East came to Jerusalem, saying, "Where is he who has been born king of the Jews? For we have seen his star in the East, and have come to worship him." When Herod the king heard this, he was troubled, and all Jerusalem with him; and assembling all the chief priests and scribes of the people, he inquired of them where the Christ was to be born. They told him, "In Bethlehem of Judea; for so it is written by the prophet: `And you, O Bethlehem, in the land of Judah, are by no means least among the rulers of Judah; for from you shall come a ruler who will govern my people Israel.'"Then Herod summoned the wise men secretly and ascertained from them what time the star appeared; and he sent them to Bethlehem, saying, "Go and search diligently for the child, and when you have found him bring me word, that I too may come and worship him." When they had heard the king they went their way; and lo, the star which they had seen in the East went before them, till it came to rest over the place where the child was. When they saw the star, they rejoiced exceedingly with great joy; and going into the house they saw the child with Mary his mother, and they fell down and worshiped him. Then, opening their treasures, they offered him gifts, gold and frankincense and myrrh. And being warned in a dream not to return to Herod, they departed to their own country by another way.

Wise men have e - ver searched for the child, they
Oth - ers would read in texts from of old, they
Then there are those who fath - om His face, and
But we who want true life for - e - ver, we

look to the stars to find Him. The ans - wer is out there,
look to the Book to find Him, be - cause they are sure that
look to a crad - le and hut, in which they can wor - ship
look in our Selves, to the soul, where - in we can list - en

the cos - mos the path to sal - va - tion will yield.
the Scrip - tures would teach them the truth long fore - told.
and of - fer their gifts at the ho - li - est place.
and ans - wer to Je - sus and His Gos - pel call.

Words: Georg Retzlaff (b. 1946)
Music: *Bamberg*, Georg Retzlaff (b. 1946)

9 8 9 8

First Sunday After the Epiphany

Matthew 3:13-17

Jesus came from Galilee to John at the Jordan, to be baptized by him. John would have prevented him, saying, "I need to be baptized by you, and do you come to me?" But Jesus answered him, "Let it be so now; for it is proper for us in this way to fulfill all righteousness." Then he consented. And when Jesus had been baptized, just as he came up from the water, suddenly the heavens were opened to him and he saw the Spirit of God descending like a dove and alighting on him. And a voice from heaven said, "This is my Son, the Beloved, with whom I am well pleased."

Words: Georg Retzlaff (b. 1946)
Music: *Ascension*, Georg Retzlaff (b. 1946)

10 5 10 5

Second Sunday After the Epiphany

John 1:29-42

John saw Jesus coming toward him and declared, "Here is the Lamb of God who takes away the sin of the world! This is he of whom I said, 'After me comes a man who ranks ahead of me because he was before me.' I myself did not know him; but I came baptizing with water for this reason, that he might be revealed to Israel." And John testified, "I saw the Spirit descending from heaven like a dove, and it remained on him. I myself did not know him, but the one who sent me to baptize with water said to me, 'He on whom you see the Spirit descend and remain is the one who baptizes with the Holy Spirit.' And I myself have seen and have testified that this is the Son of God."

The next day John again was standing with two of his disciples, and as he watched Jesus walk by, he exclaimed, "Look, here is the Lamb of God!" The two disciples heard him say this, and they followed Jesus. When Jesus turned and saw them following, he said to them, "What are you looking for?" They said to him, "Rabbi" (which translated means Teacher), "where are you staying?" He said to them, "Come and see." They came and saw where he was staying, and they remained with him that day. It was about four o'clock in the afternoon. One of the two who heard John speak and followed him was Andrew, Simon Peter's brother. He first found his brother Simon and said to him, "We have found the Messiah" (which is translated Anointed). He brought Simon to Jesus, who looked at him and said, "You are Simon son of John. You are to be called Cephas" (which is translated Peter).

Georg Retzlaff

Too long, o Lord, we were in the dark a - bout your
We sat, in prayer, ex - pec - ting a gift for deeds we
Then Truth ap - peared, in bo - di - ly form, im - mersed it
All praise to Him whose mer - cy has freed His friends from

will and your ho - ly laws. We searched and stu - died
deemed to be right-eous ness. We dread - ed wrath for
was, giv - ing life and hope to us who reeled like
sin, from no - tions of good, of me - rits earned, of

texts from of old and of - ten sinned, mis - sing goal and
fail - ure and sin, and knew that pun - ish - ment would be
stag - ger - ing men in clou - dy mists and thun - de - ring
an - ger de served, who showed us love a - part from our

mark.
swift.
storm.
deed.

Words: Georg Retzlaff (b. 1946)
Music: *Sheng En*, melody Su Yin-Lan (20th c)
HPEC 1982, 342

99 99

Third Sunday After the Epiphany

Matthew 4:12-23

When Jesus heard that John had been arrested, he withdrew to Galilee. He left Nazareth and made his home in Capernaum by the sea, in the territory of Zebulun and Naphtali, so that what had been spoken through the prophet Isaiah might be fulfilled: "Land of Zebulun, land of Naphtali, on the road by the sea, across the Jordan, Galilee of the Gentiles-- the people who sat in darkness have seen a great light, and for those who sat in the region and shadow of death light has dawned." From that time Jesus began to proclaim, "Repent, for the kingdom of heaven has come near." As he walked by the Sea of Galilee, he saw two brothers, Simon, who is called Peter, and Andrew his brother, casting a net into the sea-- for they were fishermen. And he said to them, "Follow me, and I will make you fish for people." Immediately they left their nets and followed him. As he went from there, he saw two other brothers, James son of Zebedee and his brother John, in the boat with their father Zebedee, mending their nets, and he called them. Immediately they left the boat and their father, and followed him. Jesus went throughout Galilee, teaching in their synagogues and proclaiming the good news of the kingdom and curing every disease and every sickness among the people.

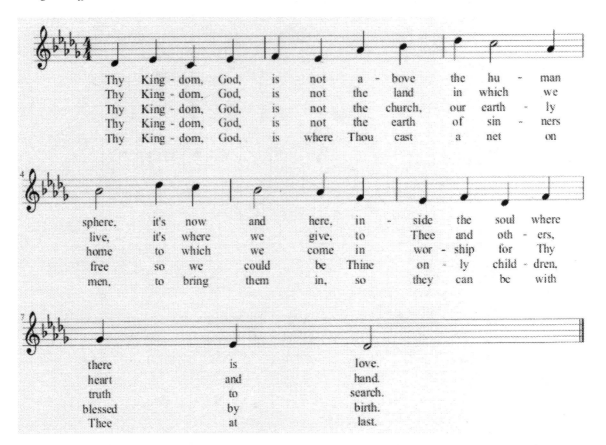

Words: Georg Retzlaff (b. 1946)
Music: *Joy Louise*, Georg Retzlaff (b. 1946)

8448

Fourth Sunday After the Epiphany

Matthew 5:1-12

When Jesus saw the crowds, he went up the mountain; and after he sat down, his disciples came to him. Then he began to speak, and taught them, saying:"Blessed are the poor in spirit, for theirs is the kingdom of heaven. "Blessed are those who mourn, for they will be comforted. "Blessed are the meek, for they will inherit the earth. "Blessed are those who hunger and thirst for righteousness, for they will be filled. "Blessed are the merciful, for they will receive mercy. "Blessed are the pure in heart, for they will see God. "Blessed are the peacemakers, for they will be called children of God. "Blessed are those who are persecuted for righteousness' sake, for theirs is the kingdom of heaven. "Blessed are you when people revile you and persecute you and utter all kinds of evil against you falsely on my account. Rejoice and be glad, for your reward is great in heaven, for in the same way they persecuted the prophets who were before you.

Why do I lis - ten, why do I care? Why do
Je - sus is speak - ing truths most pro - found, His word
This is His mes - sage: last - ing re - lease, learn to

I feel in - side me, so rare, a stir - ring of love?
is new, is di - vine and sound, my heart He does move.
be poor and pure and at peace, and yearn for a - bove.

Words: Georg Retzlaff (b. 1946)
Music: *Koniortos*, Georg Retzlaff (b. 1946)

9 9 5

Fifth Sunday After the Epiphany

Matthew 5:13-20

Jesus said, "You are the salt of the earth; but if salt has lost its taste, how can its saltiness be restored? It is no longer good for anything, but is thrown out and trampled under foot. "You are the light of the world. A city built on a hill cannot be hid. No one after lighting a lamp puts it under the bushel basket, but on the lampstand, and it gives light to all in the house. In the same way, let your light shine before others, so that they may see your good works and give glory to your Father in heaven. "Do not think that I have come to abolish the law or the prophets; I have come not to abolish but to fulfill. For truly I tell you, until heaven and earth pass away, not one letter, not one stroke of a letter, will pass from the law until all is accomplished. Therefore, whoever breaks one of the least of these commandments, and teaches others to do the same, will be called least in the kingdom of heaven; but whoever does them and teaches them will be called great in the kingdom of heaven. For I tell you, unless your righteousness exceeds that of the scribes and Pharisees, you will never enter the kingdom of heaven."

Georg Retzlaff

You will be dif-fer-ent, says the Lord, that's why I
Sea-son the dull-ness of hu-man life, stir up the
Let your light shine so oth-ers can see hea-ven-ly
Build you a ci-ty, high on a hill, vi-sib-ly

called you. Your right-eous-ness will all else ex-ceed,
tir-ed! Wa-ken the sen-ses of young and old,
glo-ry; make their lives bright, in word and in deed,
gleam-ing, eve-ry one sees and yearns for this home:

this you can now do:
new-ly in-spi-red.
tell them the Sto-ry.
church of re-dee-ming.

Words: Georg Retzlaff (b. 1946)
Music: *Retreat*, Georg Retzlaff (b. 1946)

9595

Sixth Sunday After the Epiphany

Matthew 5:21-37

Jesus said, "You have heard that it was said to those of ancient times, `You shall not murder'; and `whoever murders shall be liable to judgment.' But I say to you that if you are angry with a brother or sister, you will be liable to judgment; and if you insult a brother or sister, you will be liable to the council; and if you say, `You fool,' you will be liable to the hell of fire. So when you are offering your gift at the altar, if you remember that your brother or sister has something against you, leave your gift there before the altar and go; first be reconciled to your brother or sister, and then come and offer your gift. Come to terms quickly with your accuser while you are on the way to court with him, or your accuser may hand you over to the judge, and the judge to the guard, and you will be thrown into prison. Truly I tell you, you will never get out until you have paid the last penny. "You have heard that it was said, `You shall not commit adultery.' But I say to you that everyone who looks at a woman with lust has already committed adultery with her in his heart. If your right eye causes you to sin, tear it out and throw it away; it is better for you to lose one of your members than for your whole body to be thrown into hell. And if your right hand causes you to sin, cut it off and throw it away; it is better for you to lose one of your members than for your whole body to go into hell." It was also said, `Whoever divorces his wife, let him give her a certificate of divorce.' But I say to you that anyone who divorces his wife, except on the ground of unchastity, causes her to commit adultery; and whoever marries a divorced woman commits adultery. "Again, you have heard that it was said to those of ancient times, `You shall not swear falsely, but carry out the vows you have made to the Lord.' But I say to you, Do not swear at all, either by heaven, for it is the throne of God, or by the earth, for it is his footstool, or by Jerusalem, for it is the city of the great King. And do not swear by your head, for you cannot make one hair white or black. Let your word be `Yes, Yes' or `No, No'; anything more than this comes from the evil one.

Words: Georg Retzlaff (b. 1946)
Music: *Longfellow*, Georg Retzlaff (b. 1946)

88 88

Seventh Sunday After the Epiphany

Matthew 5:38-48

Jesus said, "You have heard that it was said, 'An eye for an eye and a tooth for a tooth.' But I say to you, Do not resist an evildoer. But if anyone strikes you on the right cheek, turn the other also; and if anyone wants to sue you and take your coat, give your cloak as well; and if anyone forces you to go one mile, go also the second mile. Give to everyone who begs from you, and do not refuse anyone who wants to borrow from you. "You have heard that it was said, 'You shall love your neighbor and hate your enemy.' But I say to you, Love your enemies and pray for those who persecute you, so that you may be children of your Father in heaven; for he makes his sun rise on the evil and on the good, and sends rain on the righteous and on the unrighteous. For if you love those who love you, what reward do you have? Do not even the tax collectors do the same? And if you greet only your brothers and sisters, what more are you doing than others? Do not even the Gentiles do the same? Be perfect, therefore, as your heavenly Father is perfect."

Georg Retzlaff

You gave us, God, a mind
To think and to reflect,
In place of cruelty
A better way to find.

You led the human race
Away from jungle law,
Where brute revenge did rule
And soiled our godly face.

You helped us look beyond
The law of eye and tooth,
Where paying back was good,
Forgiveness was not found.

Then Jesus came and taught:
The law of perfect love,
Of turning cheek, and peace
To us in mercy brought.

No we give thanks and pray
That we be instruments
Of kindness in the world
And see His Gospel day.

Words: Georg Retzlaff (b. 1946)
Music: *Eden*, Oswald Mosley Feilden, 1863

66 66

Eighth Sunday After the Epiphany

Matthew 6:24-34

Jesus said, "No one can serve two masters; for a slave will either hate the one and love the other, or be devoted to the one and despise the other. You cannot serve God and wealth." Therefore I tell you, do not worry about your life, what you will eat or what you will drink, or about your body, what you will wear. Is not life more than food, and the body more than clothing? Look at the birds of the air; they neither sow nor reap nor gather into barns, and yet your heavenly Father feeds them. Are you not of more value than they? And can any of you by worrying add a single hour to your span of life? And why do you worry about clothing? Consider the lilies of the field, how they grow; they neither toil nor spin, yet I tell you, even Solomon in all his glory was not clothed like one of these. But if God so clothes the grass of the field, which is alive today and tomorrow is thrown into the oven, will he not much more clothe you-- you of little faith? Therefore do not worry, saying, `What will we eat?' or `What will we drink?' or `What will we wear?' For it is the Gentiles who strive for all these things; and indeed your heavenly Father knows that you need all these things. But strive first for the kingdom of God and his righteousness, and all these things will be given to you as well. "So do not worry about tomorrow, for tomorrow will bring worries of its own. Today's trouble is enough for today."

Georg Retzlaff

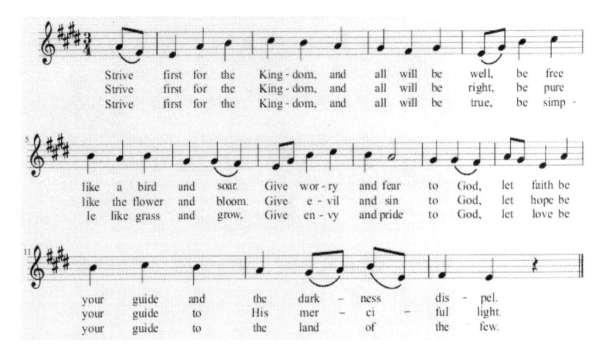

Strive first for the King-dom, and all will be well, be free
Strive first for the King-dom, and all will be right, be pure
Strive first for the King-dom, and all will be true, be simp -

like a bird and soar. Give wor-ry and fear to God, let faith be
like the flower and bloom. Give e-vil and sin to God, let hope be
le like grass and grow. Give en-vy and pride to God, let love be

your guide and the dark - ness dis - pel.
your guide to His mer - ci - ful light.
your guide to the land of the few.

Words: Georg Retzlaff (b. 1946)
Music: *Twelfth Street*, Georg Retzlaff (b. 1946)

11 77 11

34

Last Sunday After the Epiphany

Matthew 17:1-9

Six days after Peter had acknowledged Jesus as the Christ, the Son of the Living God, Jesus took with him Peter and James and his brother John and led them up a high mountain, by themselves. And he was transfigured before them, and his face shone like the sun, and his clothes became dazzling white. Suddenly there appeared to them Moses and Elijah, talking with him. Then Peter said to Jesus, "Lord, it is good for us to be here; if you wish, I will make three dwellings here, one for you, one for Moses, and one for Elijah." While he was still speaking, suddenly a bright cloud overshadowed them, and from the cloud a voice said, "This is my Son, the Beloved; with him I am well pleased; listen to him!" When the disciples heard this, they fell to the ground and were overcome by fear. But Jesus came and touched them, saying, "Get up and do not be afraid." And when they looked up, they saw no one except Jesus himself alone. As they were coming down the mountain, Jesus ordered them, "Tell no one about the vision until after the Son of Man has been raised from the dead."

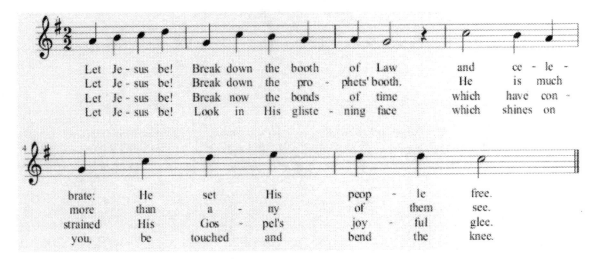

Words: Georg Retzlaff (b. 1946)
Music: *Goldfinch*, Georg Retzlaff (b. 1946)

46 46

Ash Wednesday

Matthew 6:1-6,16-21

Jesus said, "Beware of practicing your piety before others in order to be seen by them; for then you have no reward from your Father in heaven. "So whenever you give alms, do not sound a trumpet before you, as the hypocrites do in the synagogues and in the streets, so that they may be praised by others. Truly I tell you, they have received their reward. But when you give alms, do not let your left hand know what your right hand is doing, so that your alms may be done in secret; and your Father who sees in secret will reward you. "And whenever you pray, do not be like the hypocrites; for they love to stand and pray in the synagogues and at the street corners, so that they may be seen by others. Truly I tell you, they have received their reward. But whenever you pray, go into your room and shut the door and pray to your Father who is in secret; and your Father who sees in secret will reward you. "And whenever you fast, do not look dismal, like the hypocrites, for they disfigure their faces so as to show others that they are fasting. Truly I tell you, they have received their reward. But when you fast, put oil on your head and wash your face, so that your fasting may be seen not by others but by your Father who is in secret; and your Father who sees in secret will reward you. "Do not store up for yourselves treasures on earth, where moth and rust consume and where thieves break in and steal; but store up for yourselves treasures in heaven, where neither moth nor rust consumes and where thieves do not break in and steal. For where your treasure is, there your heart will be also."

Thy church, o God, is gathered
To mark these Forty Days
To cleanse our souls and bodies
And walk Thy holy ways.

Confess, my soul, that often
You give not from the heart,
But use your gift to show us
How far you are apart.

Confess, my soul, how rarely
You open prayer's room,
How alien your words are
But for the times of doom.

Confess, my soul, why deeply
You are in love with things,
That they control and own you
And clip your Spirit wings.

Thy church, o God, is gathered,
That Thou may'st wash her face,
And cleanse her from deception
By mercy and by grace.

Words: Georg Retzlaff (b. 1946)
Music: *Christus, der ist mein Leben*, melody Melchior Vulpius (1560?-1616)
HPEC 1982, 295

7676

First Sunday in Lent

Matthew 4:1-11

After Jesus was baptized, he was led up by the Spirit into the wilderness to be tempted by the devil. He fasted forty days and forty nights, and afterwards he was famished. The tempter came and said to him, "If you are the Son of God, command these stones to become loaves of bread." But he answered, "It is written, 'One does not live by bread alone, but by every word that comes from the mouth of God.'" Then the devil took him to the holy city and placed him on the pinnacle of the temple, saying to him, "If you are the Son of God, throw yourself down; for it is written, 'He will command his angels concerning you,' and 'On their hands they will bear you up, so that you will not dash your foot against a stone.'" Jesus said to him, "Again it is written, 'Do not put the Lord your God to the test.'" Again, the devil took him to a very high mountain and showed him all the kingdoms of the world and their splendor; and he said to him, "All these I will give you, if you will fall down and worship me." Jesus said to him, "Away with you, Satan! for it is written, 'Worship the Lord your God, and serve only him.'" Then the devil left him, and suddenly angels came and waited on him.

Georg Retzlaff

Words: Georg Retzlaff (b. 1946)
Music: *Wannamaker*, Georg Retzlaff (b. 1946)

87 88

Second Sunday in Lent

John 3:1-17

There was a Pharisee named Nicodemus, a leader of the Jews. He came to Jesus by night and said to him, "Rabbi, we know that you are a teacher who has come from God; for no one can do these signs that you do apart from the presence of God." Jesus answered him, "Very truly, I tell you, no one can see the kingdom of God without being born from above." Nicodemus said to him, "How can anyone be born after having grown old? Can one enter a second time into the mother's womb and be born?" Jesus answered, "Very truly, I tell you, no one can enter the kingdom of God without being born of water and Spirit. What is born of the flesh is flesh, and what is born of the Spirit is spirit. Do not be astonished that I said to you, 'You must be born from above.' The wind blows where it chooses, and you hear the sound of it, but you do not know where it comes from or where it goes. So it is with everyone who is born of the Spirit." Nicodemus said to him, "How can these things be?" Jesus answered him, "Are you a teacher of Israel, and yet you do not understand these things? "Very truly, I tell you, we speak of what we know and testify to what we have seen; yet you do not receive our testimony. If I have told you about earthly things and you do not believe, how can you believe if I tell you about heavenly things? No one has ascended into heaven except the one who descended from heaven, the Son of Man. And just as Moses lifted up the serpent in the wilderness, so must the Son of Man be lifted up, that whoever believes in him may have eternal life. "For God so loved the world that he gave his only Son, so that everyone who believes in him may not perish but may have eternal life. "Indeed, God did not send the Son into the world to condemn the world, but in order that the world might be saved through him."

Georg Retzlaff

Come unto me at night,
In hours of great distress,
When sleep does fail your eyes,
It's I who does invite.

O you who know too much,
Forget what you were told!
All those who want to know,
The hem of Truth must touch.

You can begin anew,
Like children growing up,
Discovering the wind
Again, and how it blew.

Let God's own Spirit form
Your lives to His delight.
Begin with God, and be
In love and grace reborn.

Words: Georg Retzlaff (b. 1946)
Music: *Moseley*, Henry Smart 1881
HPEC 1982, 700

66 66

Third Sunday in Lent

John 4:5-42

Jesus came to a Samaritan city called Sychar, near the plot of ground that Jacob had given to his son Joseph. Jacob's well was there, and Jesus, tired out by his journey, was sitting by the well. It was about noon. A Samaritan woman came to draw water, and Jesus said to her, "Give me a drink." (His disciples had gone to the city to buy food.) The Samaritan woman said to him, "How is it that you, a Jew, ask a drink of me, a woman of Samaria?" (Jews do not share things in common with Samaritans.) Jesus answered her, "If you knew the gift of God, and who it is that is saying to you, 'Give me a drink,' you would have asked him, and he would have given you living water." The woman said to him, "Sir, you have no bucket, and the well is deep. Where do you get that living water? Are you greater than our ancestor Jacob, who gave us the well, and with his sons and his flocks drank from it?" Jesus said to her, "Everyone who drinks of this water will be thirsty again, but those who drink of the water that I will give them will never be thirsty. The water that I will give will become in them a spring of water gushing up to eternal life." The woman said to him, "Sir, give me this water, so that I may never be thirsty or have to keep coming here to draw water."Jesus said to her, "Go, call your husband, and come back." The woman answered him, "I have no husband." Jesus said to her, "You are right in saying, 'I have no husband'; for you have had five husbands, and the one you have now is not your husband. What you have said is true!" The woman said to him, "Sir, I see that you are a prophet. Our ancestors worshiped on this mountain, but you say that the place where people must worship is in Jerusalem." Jesus said to her, "Woman, believe me, the hour is coming when you will worship the Father neither on this mountain nor in Jerusalem. You worship what you do not know; we worship what we know, for salvation is from the Jews. But the hour is coming, and is now here, when the true worshipers will worship the Father in spirit and truth, for the Father seeks such as these to worship him. God is spirit, and those who worship him must worship in spirit and truth." The woman said to him, "I know that Messiah is coming" (who is called Christ). "When he comes, he will proclaim all things to us." Jesus said to her, "I am he, the one who is speaking to you." Just then his disciples came. They were astonished that he was speaking with a woman, but no one said, "What do you want?" or, "Why are you speaking with her?" Then the woman left her water jar and went back to the city. She said to the people, "Come and see a man who told me everything I have ever done! He cannot be the Messiah, can he?" They left the city and were on their way to him. Meanwhile the disciples were urging him, "Rabbi, eat something." But he said to them, "I have food to eat that you do not know about." So the disciples said to one another, "Surely no one has brought him something to eat?" Jesus said to them, "My food is to do the will of him who sent me and to complete his work. Do you not say, `Four months more, then comes the harvest'? But I tell you, look around you, and see how the fields are ripe for harvesting. The reaper is already receiving wages and is gathering fruit for eternal life, so that sower and reaper may rejoice together. For here the saying holds true, `One sows and another reaps.' I sent you to reap that for which you did not labor. Others have labored, and you have entered into their labor." Many Samaritans from that city believed in him because of the woman's testimony, "He told me everything I have ever done." So when the Samaritans came to him, they asked him to stay with them; and he stayed there two days. And many more believed because of his word. They said to the woman, "It is no longer because of what you said that we believe, for we have heard for ourselves, and we know that this is truly the Savior of the world."

Come, worship the Father in Spirit and Truth,
Leave lands, plains, and mountains, and seek Him within!
Learn that the Redeemer will meet you at home,
In silence will touch you, restore you to youth.

Come, drink from the well-spring the water of life,
Leave race, pride, and people, and stand before God
Alone, poor, and guilty, in need of His Word
To bless you and heal you and end all your strife.

Come, speak now to others and share the Good News,
Leave cowardice, fear, let timidity go,
And boldly proclaim, both in words and in deeds:
It's Jesus who chose us, and Him do we choose.

Words: Georg Retzlaff (b. 1946)
Music: *St. Denio*, Welsh hymn, from Caniadau y Cyssegr, 1839
HPEC 1982, 423

11 11 11 11

Fourth Sunday in Lent

John 9:1-41

As he walked along, he saw a man blind from birth. His disciples asked him, "Rabbi, who sinned, this man or his parents, that he was born blind?" Jesus answered, "Neither this man nor his parents sinned; he was born blind so that God's works might be revealed in him. We must work the works of him who sent me while it is day; night is coming when no one can work. As long as I am in the world, I am the light of the world." When he had said this, he spat on the ground and made mud with the saliva and spread the mud on the man's eyes, saying to him, "Go, wash in the pool of Siloam" (which means Sent). Then he went and washed and came back able to see. The neighbors and those who had seen him before as a beggar began to ask, "Is this not the man who used to sit and beg?" Some were saying, "It is he." Others were saying, "No, but it is someone like him." He kept saying, "I am the man." But they kept asking him, "Then how were your eyes opened?" He answered, "The man called Jesus made mud, spread it on my eyes, and said to me, 'Go to Siloam and wash.' Then I went and washed and received my sight." They said to him, "Where is he?" He said, "I do not know." They brought to the Pharisees the man who had formerly been blind. Now it was a sabbath day when Jesus made the mud and opened his eyes. Then the Pharisees also began to ask him how he had received his sight. He said to them, "He put mud on my eyes. Then I washed, and now I see." Some of the Pharisees said, "This man is not from God, for he does not observe the sabbath." But others said, "How can a man who is a sinner perform such signs?" And they were divided. So they said again to the blind man, "What do you say about him? It was your eyes he opened." He said, "He is a prophet." The Jews did not believe that he had been blind and had received his sight until they called the parents of the man who had received his sight and asked them, "Is this your son, who you say was born blind? How then does he now see?" His parents answered, "We know that this is our son, and that he was born blind; but we do not know how it is that now he sees, nor do we know who opened his eyes. Ask him; he is of age. He will speak for himself." His parents said this because they were afraid of the Jews; for the Jews had already agreed that anyone who confessed Jesus to be the Messiah would be put out of the synagogue. Therefore his parents said, "He is of age; ask him." So for the second time they called the man who had been blind, and they said to him, "Give glory to God! We know that this man is a sinner." He answered, "I do not know whether he is a sinner. One thing I do know, that though I was blind, now I see." They said to him, "What did he do to you? How did he open your eyes?" He answered them, "I have told you already, and you would not listen. Why do you want to hear it again? Do you also want to become his disciples?" Then they reviled him, saying, "You are his disciple, but we are disciples of Moses. We know that God has spoken to Moses, but as for this man, we do not know where he comes from." The man answered, "Here is an astonishing thing! You do not know where he comes from, and yet he opened my eyes. We know that God does not listen to sinners, but he does listen to one who worships him and obeys his will. Never since the world began has it been heard that anyone opened the eyes of a person born blind. If this man were not from God, he could do nothing." They answered him, "You were born entirely in sins, and are you trying to teach us?" And they drove him out. Jesus heard that they had driven him out, and when he found him, he said, "Do you believe in the Son of Man?" He answered, "And who is he, sir? Tell me, so that I may believe in him." Jesus said to him, "You have seen him, and the one speaking with you is he." He said, "Lord, I believe." And he worshiped him. Jesus said, "I came into this world for judgment so that those who do not see may see, and those who do see may become blind." Some of the Pharisees near him heard this and said to him, "Surely we are not blind, are we?" Jesus said to them, "If you were blind, you would not have sin. But now that you say, `We see,' your sin remains."

Georg Retzlaff

In life's arduous journey much
Suffering and pain abound.
Answers, reasons can't be found
Unless we wash our eyes.

Is it God who punishes,
Separates the dross from gold?
Meaning, purpose can't be told
Unless we wash our eyes.

Does the Father send a test
For our faith, or does He teach?
Nowhere near the Truth we reach
Unless we wash our eyes.

To Siloam go and wash,
See anew what God reveals,
Who your fathers' sins repeals,
To Him be all the praise!

Words: Georg Retzlaff (b. 1946)
Music: *Holy Comfort*, R.S. Genge
EH 1933, 410

77 76

Fifth Sunday in Lent

John 11:1-45

Now a certain man was ill, Lazarus of Bethany, the village of Mary and her sister Martha. Mary was the one who anointed the Lord with perfume and wiped his feet with her hair; her brother Lazarus was ill. So the sisters sent a message to Jesus, "Lord, he whom you love is ill." But when Jesus heard it, he said, "This illness does not lead to death; rather it is for God's glory, so that the Son of God may be glorified through it." Accordingly, though Jesus loved Martha and her sister and Lazarus, after having heard that Lazarus was ill, he stayed two days longer in the place where he was. Then after this he said to the disciples, "Let us go to Judea again." The disciples said to him, "Rabbi, the Jews were just now trying to stone you, and are you going there again?" Jesus answered, "Are there not twelve hours of daylight? Those who walk during the day do not stumble, because they see the light of this world. But those who walk at night stumble, because the light is not in them." After saying this, he told them, "Our friend Lazarus has fallen asleep, but I am going there to awaken him." The disciples said to him, "Lord, if he has fallen asleep, he will be all right." Jesus, however, had been speaking about his death, but they thought that he was referring merely to sleep. Then Jesus told them plainly, "Lazarus is dead. For your sake I am glad I was not there, so that you may believe. But let us go to him." Thomas, who was called the Twin, said to his fellow disciples, "Let us also go, that we may die with him." When Jesus arrived, he found that Lazarus had already been in the tomb four days. Now Bethany was near Jerusalem, some two miles away, and many of the Jews had come to Martha and Mary to console them about their brother. When Martha heard that Jesus was coming, she went and met him, while Mary stayed at home. Martha said to Jesus, "Lord, if you had been here, my brother would not have died. But even now I know that God will give you whatever you ask of him." Jesus said to her, "Your brother will rise again." Martha said to him, "I know that he will rise again in the resurrection on the last day." Jesus said to her, "I am the resurrection and the life. Those who believe in me, even though they die, will live, and everyone who lives and believes in me will never die. Do you believe this?" She said to him, "Yes, Lord, I believe that you are the Messiah, the Son of God, the one coming into the world." When she had said this, she went back and called her sister Mary, and told her privately, "The Teacher is here and is calling for you." And when she heard it, she got up quickly and went to him. Now Jesus had not yet come to the village, but was still at the place where Martha had met him. The Jews who were with her in the house, consoling her, saw Mary get up quickly and go out. They followed her because they thought that she was going to the tomb to weep there. When Mary came where Jesus was and saw him, she knelt at his feet and said to him, "Lord, if you had been here, my brother would not have died." When Jesus saw her weeping, and the Jews who came with her also weeping, he was greatly disturbed in spirit and deeply moved. He said, "Where have you laid him?" They said to him, "Lord, come and see." Jesus began to weep. So the Jews said, "See how he loved him!" But some of them said, "Could not he who opened the eyes of the blind man have kept this man from dying?" Then Jesus, again greatly disturbed, came to the tomb. It was a cave, and a stone was lying against it. Jesus said, "Take away the stone." Martha, the sister of the dead man, said to him, "Lord, already there is a stench because he has been dead four days." Jesus said to her, "Did I not tell you that if you believed, you would see the glory of God?" So they took away the stone. And Jesus looked upward and said, "Father, I thank you for having heard me. I knew that you always hear me, but I have said this for the sake of the crowd standing here, so that they may believe that you sent me." When he had said this, he cried with a loud voice, "Lazarus, come out!" The dead man came out, his hands and feet bound with strips of cloth, and his face wrapped in a cloth. Jesus said to them, "Unbind him, and let him go." Many of the Jews therefore, who had come with Mary and had seen what Jesus did, believed in him.

Death holds no terror for those who believed.
Gateway, a transition, a gentle return:
Peace from of old - neither grave nor the urn
Troubles the dying, or harms the bereaved.

Jesus is there, compassionate love,
Shared with the mourning, defeats all our doubt,
Moves human hearts and casts misery out,
Helps feeble minds to go far and above.

Now is the time for believers to rise
Out of their tombs and their cloths to unbind,
His resurrection and life they shall find
Deep in their souls: both the promise and prize.

Words: Georg Retzlaff (b. 1946)
Music: *Slane*, Irish ballad melody
HPEC 1982, 482

10 10 10 10

Sunday of the Passion: Palm Sunday

Matthew 21:1-11

When Jesus and his disciples had come near Jerusalem and had reached Bethphage, at the Mount of Olives, Jesus sent two disciples, saying to them, "Go into the village ahead of you, and immediately you will find a donkey tied, and a colt with her; untie them and bring them to me. If anyone says anything to you, just say this, 'The Lord needs them.' And he will send them immediately." This took place to fulfill what had been spoken through the prophet, saying, "Tell the daughter of Zion, Look, your king is coming to you, humble, and mounted on a donkey, and on a colt, the foal of a donkey." The disciples went and did as Jesus had directed them; they brought the donkey and the colt, and put their cloaks on them, and he sat on them. A very large crowd spread their cloaks on the road, and others cut branches from the trees and spread them on the road. The crowds that went ahead of him and that followed were shouting, "Hosanna to the Son of David! Blessed is the one who comes in the name of the Lord! Hosanna in the highest heaven!" When he entered Jerusalem, the whole city was in turmoil, asking, "Who is this?" The crowds were saying, "This is the prophet Jesus from Nazareth in Galilee."

What we have we bring:
Neither sword nor bow,
Branches, cloaks, instead-
Honor to our King!

What we know we sing:
Songs of peace and hope,
Not the shouts of war-
Honor to our King!

What we need, one thing:
Humble beast, a colt,
Not the horse's pride-
Honor to our King!

What, on entering
Human souls and hearts,
Has He not transformed?
Honor to our King!

Words: Georg Retzlaff (b. 1946)
Music: *Haslemere*, Songs and Tunes for Education, 1861; harm. Martin Shaw, 1931
HPEC 1940, 244

5 5 5 5

Maundy Thursday

John 13:1-17, 31b-35

Now before the festival of the Passover, Jesus knew that his hour had come to depart from this world and go to the Father. Having loved his own who were in the world, he loved them to the end. The devil had already put it into the heart of Judas son of Simon Iscariot to betray him. And during supper Jesus, knowing that the Father had given all things into his hands, and that he had come from God and was going to God, got up from the table, took off his outer robe, and tied a towel around himself. Then he poured water into a basin and began to wash the disciples' feet and to wipe them with the towel that was tied around him. He came to Simon Peter, who said to him, "Lord, are you going to wash my feet?" Jesus answered, "You do not know now what I am doing, but later you will understand." Peter said to him, "You will never wash my feet." Jesus answered, "Unless I wash you, you have no share with me." Simon Peter said to him, "Lord, not my feet only but also my hands and my head!" Jesus said to him, "One who has bathed does not need to wash, except for the feet, but is entirely clean. And you are clean, though not all of you." For he knew who was to betray him; for this reason he said, "Not all of you are clean." After he had washed their feet, had put on his robe, and had returned to the table, he said to them, "Do you know what I have done to you? You call me Teacher and Lord--and you are right, for that is what I am. So if I, your Lord and Teacher, have washed your feet, you also ought to wash one another's feet. For I have set you an example, that you also should do as I have done to you. Very truly, I tell you, servants are not greater than their master, nor are messengers greater than the one who sent them. If you know these things, you are blessed if you do them. Jesus said, "Now the Son of Man has been glorified, and God has been glorified in him. If God has been glorified in him, God will also glorify him in himself and will glorify him at once. Little children, I am with you only a little longer. You will look for me; and as I said to the Jews so now I say to you, `Where I am going, you cannot come.' I give you a new commandment, that you love one another. Just as I have loved you, you also should love one another. By this everyone will know that you are my disciples, if you have love for one another."

As Christ's one body have we come together
To offer worship, lifting our voices
With all the Saints in regions high and nether:
Kyrie eleison.

His blood and body call us to remember
The living Savior and His holy gospel,
His saving grace for each and every member:
Christe eleison.

To you be glory, God, who consecrated
All of your creatures, pouring out your Spirit,
To make one body all you have created:
Kyrie eleison.

Words: Georg Retzlaff (b. 1946)
Music: *Mighty Savior*, David Hurd (b. 1950)
HPEC 1982, 35

11 11 11 7

Good Friday

John 18:1-19:42

After Jesus had spoken these words, he went out with his disciples across the Kidron valley to a place where there was a garden, which he and his disciples entered. Now Judas, who betrayed him, also knew the place, because Jesus often met there with his disciples. So Judas brought a detachment of soldiers together with police from the chief priests and the Pharisees, and they came there with lanterns and torches and weapons. Then Jesus, knowing all that was to happen to him, came forward and asked them, "Whom are you looking for?" They answered, "Jesus of Nazareth." Jesus replied, "I am he." Judas, who betrayed him, was standing with them. When Jesus said to them, "I am he," they stepped back and fell to the ground. Again he asked them, "Whom are you looking for?" And they said, "Jesus of Nazareth." Jesus answered, "I told you that I am he. So if you are looking for me, let these men go." This was to fulfill the word that he had spoken, "I did not lose a single one of those whom you gave me." Then Simon Peter, who had a sword, drew it, struck the high priest's slave, and cut off his right ear. The slave's name was Malchus. Jesus said to Peter, "Put your sword back into its sheath. Am I not to drink the cup that the Father has given me?" So the soldiers, their officer, and the Jewish police arrested Jesus and bound him. First they took him to Annas, who was the father-in-law of Caiaphas, the high priest that year. Caiaphas was the one who had advised the Jews that it was better to have one person die for the people. Simon Peter and another disciple followed Jesus. Since that disciple was known to the high priest, he went with Jesus into the courtyard of the high priest, but Peter was standing outside at the gate. So the other disciple, who was known to the high priest, went out, spoke to the woman who guarded the gate, and brought Peter in. The woman said to Peter, "You are not also one of this man's disciples, are you?" He said, "I am not." Now the slaves and the police had made a charcoal fire because it was cold, and they were standing around it and warming themselves. Peter also was standing with them and warming himself. Then the high priest questioned Jesus about his disciples and about his teaching. Jesus answered, "I have spoken openly to the world; I have always taught in synagogues and in the temple, where all the Jews come together. I have said nothing in secret. Why do you ask me? Ask those who heard what I said to them; they know what I said." When he had said this, one of the police standing nearby struck Jesus on the face, saying, "Is that how you answer the high priest?" Jesus answered, "If I have spoken wrongly, testify to the wrong. But if I have spoken rightly, why do you strike me?" Then Annas sent him bound to Caiaphas the high priest. Now Simon Peter was standing and warming himself. They asked him, "You are not also one of his disciples, are you?" He denied it and said, "I am not." One of the slaves of the high priest, a relative of the man whose ear Peter had cut off, asked, "Did I not see you in the garden with him?" Again Peter denied it, and at that moment the cock crowed. Then they took Jesus from Caiaphas to Pilate's headquarters. It was early in the morning. They themselves did not enter the headquarters, so as to avoid ritual defilement and to be able to eat the Passover. So Pilate went out to them and said, "What accusation do you bring against this man?" They answered, "If this man were not a criminal, we would not have handed him over to you." Pilate said to them, "Take him yourselves and judge him according to your law." The Jews replied, "We are not permitted to put anyone to death." (This was to fulfill what Jesus had said when he indicated the kind of death he was to die.) Then Pilate entered the headquarters again, summoned Jesus, and asked him, "Are you the King of the Jews?" Jesus answered, "Do you ask this on your own, or did others tell you about me?" Pilate replied, "I am not a Jew, am I? Your own nation and the chief priests have handed you over to me. What have you done?" Jesus answered, "My kingdom is not from this world. If my kingdom were from this world, my followers would be fighting to keep me from being handed over to the Jews. But as it is, my kingdom is not from here." Pilate asked him, "So you are a king?" Jesus answered, "You say that I am a king. For this I was born, and for this I came into the world, to testify to the truth. Everyone who belongs to the truth listens to my voice." Pilate asked him, "What is truth?" After he had said this, he went out to the Jews again and told them, "I find no case against him. But you have a custom that I release someone for you at the Passover. Do you want me to release for you the King of the Jews?" They shouted in reply, "Not this man, but Barabbas!" Now Barabbas was a bandit. Then Pilate took Jesus and had him flogged. And the soldiers wove a crown of thorns and put it on his head, and they dressed him in a purple robe. They kept coming up to him, saying, "Hail, King of the Jews!" and striking him on the face. Pilate went out again and said to them, "Look, I am bringing him out to you to let you know that I find no case against him." So Jesus came out, wearing the crown of thorns and the purple robe. Pilate said to them,

"Here is the man!" When the chief priests and the police saw him, they shouted, "Crucify him! Crucify him!" Pilate said to them, "Take him yourselves and crucify him; I find no case against him." The Jews answered him, "We have a law, and according to that law he ought to die because he has claimed to be the Son of God." Now when Pilate heard this, he was more afraid than ever. He entered his headquarters again and asked Jesus, "Where are you from?" But Jesus gave him no answer. Pilate therefore said to him, "Do you refuse to speak to me? Do you not know that I have power to release you, and power to crucify you?" Jesus answered him, "You would have no power over me unless it had been given you from above; therefore the one who handed me over to you is guilty of a greater sin." From then on Pilate tried to release him, but the Jews cried out, "If you release this man, you are no friend of the emperor. Everyone who claims to be a king sets himself against the emperor." When Pilate heard these words, he brought Jesus outside and sat on the judge's bench at a place called The Stone Pavement, or in Hebrew Gabbatha. Now it was the day of Preparation for the Passover; and it was about noon. He said to the Jews, "Here is your King!" They cried out, "Away with him! Away with him! Crucify him!" Pilate asked them, "Shall I crucify your King?" The chief priests answered, "We have no king but the emperor." Then he handed him over to them to be crucified. So they took Jesus; and carrying the cross by himself, he went out to what is called The Place of the Skull, which in Hebrew is called Golgotha. There they crucified him, and with him two others, one on either side, with Jesus between them. Pilate also had an inscription written and put on the cross. It read, "Jesus of Nazareth, the King of the Jews." Many of the Jews read this inscription, because the place where Jesus was crucified was near the city; and it was written in Hebrew, in Latin, and in Greek. Then the chief priests of the Jews said to Pilate, "Do not write, 'The King of the Jews,' but, 'This man said, I am King of the Jews.'" Pilate answered, "What I have written I have written." When the soldiers had crucified Jesus, they took his clothes and divided them into four parts, one for each soldier. They also took his tunic; now the tunic was seamless, woven in one piece from the top. So they said to one another, "Let us not tear it, but cast lots for it to see who will get it." This was to fulfill what the scripture says, "They divided my clothes among themselves, and for my clothing they cast lots." And that is what the soldiers did. Meanwhile, standing near the cross of Jesus were his mother, and his mother's sister, Mary the wife of Clopas, and Mary Magdalene. When Jesus saw his mother and the disciple whom he loved standing beside her, he said to his mother, "Woman, here is your son." Then he said to the disciple, "Here is your mother." And from that hour the disciple took her into his own home. After this, when Jesus knew that all was now finished, he said (in order to fulfill the scripture), "I am thirsty." A jar full of sour wine was standing there. So they put a sponge full of the wine on a branch of hyssop and held it to his mouth. When Jesus had received the wine, he said, "It is finished." Then he bowed his head and gave up his spirit. Since it was the day of Preparation, the Jews did not want the bodies left on the cross during the sabbath, especially because that sabbath was a day of great solemnity. So they asked Pilate to have the legs of the crucified men broken and the bodies removed. Then the soldiers came and broke the legs of the first and of the other who had been crucified with him. But when they came to Jesus and saw that he was already dead, they did not break his legs. Instead, one of the soldiers pierced his side with a spear, and at once blood and water came out. (He who saw this has testified so that you also may believe. His testimony is true, and he knows that he tells the truth.) These things occurred so that the scripture might be fulfilled, "None of his bones shall be broken." And again another passage of scripture says, "They will look on the one whom they have pierced." After these things, Joseph of Arimathea, who was a disciple of Jesus, though a secret one because of his fear of the Jews, asked Pilate to let him take away the body of Jesus. Pilate gave him permission; so he came and removed his body. Nicodemus, who had at first come to Jesus by night, also came, bringing a mixture of myrrh and aloes, weighing about a hundred pounds. They took the body of Jesus and wrapped it with the spices in linen cloths, according to the burial custom of the Jews. Now there was a garden in the place where he was crucified, and in the garden there was a new tomb in which no one had ever been laid. And so, because it was the Jewish day of Preparation, and the tomb was nearby, they laid Jesus there.

For us you died a death to wake us all,
we thank you, Lord!
From everlasting sleep,
From careless lives and deep
Despairing days and nights
Of fears and painful frights.
For us you died a death to wake us all,
we thank you, Lord!

For us you died a death to wake us all,
we thank you, Lord!
You gave your body, life,
And love you showed in strife
Against your enemy.
And those who follow see:
For us you died a death to wake us all,
we thank you, Lord!

For us you died a death to wake us all,
we thank you, Lord!
You ended hopelessness,
Defeated cowardice,
You were the first to fight
The battle with your might.
For us you died a death to wake us all,
we thank you, Lord!

For us you died a death to wake us all,
we thank you, Lord!
You opened our eyes
To help us see the lies
We tell to hide the truth
About ourselves from youth.
For us you died a death to wake us all,
we thank you, Lord!

Words: Georg Retzlaff (b. 1946)
Music: *High Road*, Martin Shaw
EH 1933, 427

10.4.66.66.10.4

The Great Vigil of Easter

Matthew 28:1-10

After the sabbath, as the first day of the week was dawning, Mary Magdalene and the other Mary went to see the tomb. And suddenly there was a great earthquake; for an angel of the Lord, descending from heaven, came and rolled back the stone and sat on it. His appearance was like lightning, and his clothing white as snow. For fear of him the guards shook and became like dead men. But the angel said to the women, "Do not be afraid; I know that you are looking for Jesus who was crucified. He is not here; for he has been raised, as he said. Come, see the place where he lay. Then go quickly and tell his disciples, 'He has been raised from the dead, and indeed he is going ahead of you to Galilee; there you will see him.' This is my message for you." So they left the tomb quickly with fear and great joy, and ran to tell his disciples. Suddenly Jesus met them and said, "Greetings!" And they came to him, took hold of his feet, and worshiped him. Then Jesus said to them, "Do not be afraid; go and tell my brothers to go to Galilee; there they will see me."

Let all the earth shake at the news of this morn - ing,
Let armed men be come like the dead who are bur - ied,
Let pi - ous folk fall on their knees and do hom - age,

let all the hills quake at the break of this dawn - ing:
let wo - men be dumb, at the an - gel's voice wor - ried:
let who hear the call share with oth - ers the mes - sage:

The Lord is with - in us, He speaks and He lives!

Words: Georg Retzlaff (b. 1946)
Music: *St. Elisabeth*, Georg Retzlaff (b. 1946)

57 57 65

Easter Day

John 20:1-18

Early on the first day of the week, while it was still dark, Mary Magdalene came to the tomb and saw that the stone had been removed from the tomb. So she ran and went to Simon Peter and the other disciple, the one whom Jesus loved, and said to them, "They have taken the Lord out of the tomb, and we do not know where they have laid him." Then Peter and the other disciple set out and went toward the tomb. The two were running together, but the other disciple outran Peter and reached the tomb first. He bent down to look in and saw the linen wrappings lying there, but he did not go in. Then Simon Peter came, following him, and went into the tomb. He saw the linen wrappings lying there, and the cloth that had been on Jesus' head, not lying with the linen wrappings but rolled up in a place by itself. Then the other disciple, who reached the tomb first, also went in, and he saw and believed; for as yet they did not understand the scripture, that he must rise from the dead. Then the disciples returned to their homes.

But Mary stood weeping outside the tomb. As she wept, she bent over to look into the tomb; and she saw two angels in white, sitting where the body of Jesus had been lying, one at the head and the other at the feet. They said to her, "Woman, why are you weeping?" She said to them, "They have taken away my Lord, and I do not know where they have laid him." When she had said this, she turned around and saw Jesus standing there, but she did not know that it was Jesus. Jesus said to her, "Woman, why are you weeping? Whom are you looking for?" Supposing him to be the gardener, she said to him, "Sir, if you have carried him away, tell me where you have laid him, and I will take him away." Jesus said to her, "Mary!" She turned and said to him in Hebrew, "Rabbouni!" (which means Teacher). Jesus said to her, "Do not hold on to me, because I have not yet ascended to the Father. But go to my brothers and say to them, 'I am ascending to my Father and your Father, to my God and your God.'" Mary Magdalene went and announced to the disciples, "I have seen the Lord"; and she told them that he had said these things to her.

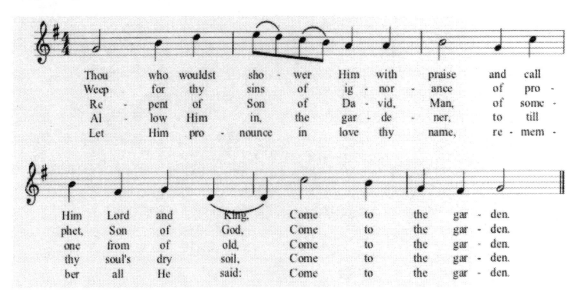

Words: Georg Retzlaff (b. 1946)
Music: *St. Clemens*, Georg Retzlaff (b. 1946)

8 6 5

Second Sunday of Easter

John 20:19-31

When it was evening on that day, the first day of the week, and the doors of the house where the disciples had met were locked for fear of the Jews, Jesus came and stood among them and said, "Peace be with you." After he said this, he showed them his hands and his side. Then the disciples rejoiced when they saw the Lord. Jesus said to them again, "Peace be with you. As the Father has sent me, so I send you." When he had said this, he breathed on them and said to them, "Receive the Holy Spirit. If you forgive the sins of any, they are forgiven them; if you retain the sins of any, they are retained." But Thomas (who was called the Twin), one of the twelve, was not with them when Jesus came. So the other disciples told him, "We have seen the Lord." But he said to them, "Unless I see the mark of the nails in his hands, and put my finger in the mark of the nails and my hand in his side, I will not believe." A week later his disciples were again in the house, and Thomas was with them. Although the doors were shut, Jesus came and stood among them and said, "Peace be with you." Then he said to Thomas, "Put your finger here and see my hands. Reach out your hand and put it in my side. Do not doubt but believe." Thomas answered him, "My Lord and my God!" Jesus said to him, "Have you believed because you have seen me? Blessed are those who have not seen and yet have come to believe." Now Jesus did many other signs in the presence of his disciples, which are not written in this book. But these are written so that you may come to believe that Jesus is the Messiah, the Son of God, and that through believing you may have life in his name.

My Lord and my God: we glad - ly pro claim words,
Our fail - ure to join with friends in their fear, to
Our plea for your peace which fills not our heart, where
My Lord and my God: you heard our re - quest, and

born out of doubt, to hon - or your Name;
walk our own path: we ask you to hear
ran - co - rous thought does poi - son and smart.
gran - ted us faith, in trust - ing you, rest.

Words: Georg Retzlaff (b. 1946)
Music: *Sullivan*, Georg Retzlaff (b. 1946)

55 55

Third Sunday of Easter

Luke 24:13-35

That very day, the first day of the week, two of the disciples were going to a village called Emmaus, about seven miles from Jerusalem, and talking with each other about all these things that had happened. While they were talking and discussing, Jesus himself came near and went with them, but their eyes were kept from recognizing him. And he said to them, "What are you discussing with each other while you walk along?" They stood still, looking sad. Then one of them, whose name was Cleopas, answered him, "Are you the only stranger in Jerusalem who does not know the things that have taken place there in these days?" He asked them, "What things?" They replied, "The things about Jesus of Nazareth, who was a prophet mighty in deed and word before God and all the people, and how our chief priests and leaders handed him over to be condemned to death and crucified him. But we had hoped that he was the one to redeem Israel. Yes, and besides all this, it is now the third day since these things took place. Moreover, some women of our group astounded us. They were at the tomb early this morning, and when they did not find his body there, they came back and told us that they had indeed seen a vision of angels who said that he was alive. Some of those who were with us went to the tomb and found it just as the women had said; but they did not see him." Then he said to them, "Oh, how foolish you are, and how slow of heart to believe all that the prophets have declared! Was it not necessary that the Messiah should suffer these things and then enter into his glory?" Then beginning with Moses and all the prophets, he interpreted to them the things about himself in all the scriptures. As they came near the village to which they were going, he walked ahead as if he were going on. But they urged him strongly, saying, "Stay with us, because it is almost evening and the day is now nearly over." So he went in to stay with them. When he was at the table with them, he took bread, blessed and broke it, and gave it to them. Then their eyes were opened, and they recognized him; and he vanished from their sight. They said to each other, "Were not our hearts burning within us while he was talking to us on the road, while he was opening the scriptures to us?" That same hour they got up and returned to Jerusalem; and they found the eleven and their companions gathered together. They were saying, "The Lord has risen indeed, and he has appeared to Simon!" Then they told what had happened on the road, and how he had been made known to them in the breaking of the bread.

Georg Retzlaff

On the roads of life we see com - pan - ions join our
Far the great - est joy of all is Jes - sus by our
It is not in text or book that Eas - ter faith is
When you feel the burn - ing heart, as words your soul do

way: par - ents, tea - chers, sib - lings, we shall wel - come
side, tel - ling us of scrip - ture's call, yet in Him
found! Break the bread and to Him look who healed your
find, make Him Lord, set Him a - part, and at His

ev-ery day.
to a - bide.
ev-ery wound.
ta-ble dine.

Words: Georg Retzlaff (b. 1946)
Music: *Aedan*, Georg Retzlaff (b. 1946)

76 76

Fourth Sunday of Easter

John 10:1-10

Jesus said, "Very truly, I tell you, anyone who does not enter the sheepfold by the gate but climbs in by another way is a thief and a bandit. The one who enters by the gate is the shepherd of the sheep. The gatekeeper opens the gate for him, and the sheep hear his voice. He calls his own sheep by name and leads them out. When he has brought out all his own, he goes ahead of them, and the sheep follow him because they know his voice. They will not follow a stranger, but they will run from him because they do not know the voice of strangers." Jesus used this figure of speech with them, but they did not understand what he was saying to them.

So again Jesus said to them, "Very truly, I tell you, I am the gate for the sheep. All who came before me are thieves and bandits; but the sheep did not listen to them. I am the gate. Whoever enters by me will be saved, and will come in and go out and find pasture. The thief comes only to steal and kill and destroy. I came that they may have life, and have it abundantly."

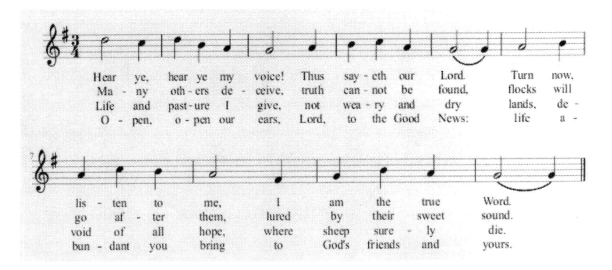

Words: Georg Retzlaff (b. 1946)
Music: *Alaena*, Georg Retzlaff (b. 1946)

65 65

Fifth Sunday of Easter

John 14:1-14

Jesus said, "Do not let your hearts be troubled. Believe in God, believe also in me. In my Father's house there are many dwelling places. If it were not so, would I have told you that I go to prepare a place for you? And if I go and prepare a place for you, I will come again and will take you to myself, so that where I am, there you may be also. And you know the way to the place where I am going." Thomas said to him, "Lord, we do not know where you are going. How can we know the way?" Jesus said to him, "I am the way, and the truth, and the life. No one comes to the Father except through me. If you know me, you will know my Father also. From now on you do know him and have seen him." Philip said to him, "Lord, show us the Father, and we will be satisfied." Jesus said to him, "Have I been with you all this time, Philip, and you still do not know me? Whoever has seen me has seen the Father. How can you say, `Show us the Father'? Do you not believe that I am in the Father and the Father is in me? The words that I say to you I do not speak on my own; but the Father who dwells in me does his works. Believe me that I am in the Father and the Father is in me; but if you do not, then believe me because of the works themselves. Very truly, I tell you, the one who believes in me will also do the works that I do and, in fact, will do greater works than these, because I am going to the Father. I will do whatever you ask in my name, so that the Father may be glorified in the Son. If in my name you ask me for anything, I will do it."

I am the Way, let it ring out!
Ye faithful sing about the path
of life which leads you home
to where you want to be.

I am the Truth, let it ring out!
All ye who yearn to know and grow
in understanding and
in simple faithfulness.

I am the Life, let it ring out!
Ye who would want to live a life
reach deep and turn around
Before it is too late.

There is a room, let it ring out,
where those we loved have gone before,
and there we, too, shall be
one day, in peace and joy.

Words: Georg Retzlaff (b. 1946)
Music: *In My Father's House: In Memory of Melton Priester*, John Lee, 2011

88 66

Sixth Sunday of Easter

John 14:15-21

Jesus said to his disciples, "If you love me, you will keep my commandments. And I will ask the Father, and he will give you another Advocate, to be with you forever. This is the Spirit of truth, whom the world cannot receive, because it neither sees him nor knows him. You know him, because he abides with you, and he will be in you.

"I will not leave you orphaned; I am coming to you. In a little while the world will no longer see me, but you will see me; because I live, you also will live. On that day you will know that I am in my Father, and you in me, and I in you. They who have my commandments and keep them are those who love me; and those who love me will be loved by my Father, and I will love them and reveal myself to them."

Come, Spirit of Truth, enlighten us who live in this
Come, Spirit of Truth, give honesty to hearts and minds
Come, Spirit of Truth, the gift of Him who made us children
Come, Spirit of Truth, the Advocate, who pleads, within

world of lies, surrounded by treason and deceit
of your friends, and free every soul from sin and death
of God, by doing away with book and law,
and above, for us to be faithful, true and good,

we yearn for that which abides.
until to you it ascends.
He showed us love as the code.
and bless this world with His love.

Words: Georg Retzlaff (b. 1946)
Music: *Terese*, Georg Retzlaff (b. 1946)

97 97

Ascension Day

Luke 24:44-53

Jesus said to his disciples, "These are my words that I spoke to you while I was still with you-- that everything written about me in the law of Moses, the prophets, and the psalms must be fulfilled." Then he opened their minds to understand the scriptures, and he said to them, "Thus it is written, that the Messiah is to suffer and to rise from the dead on the third day, and that repentance and forgiveness of sins is to be proclaimed in his name to all nations, beginning from Jerusalem. You are witnesses of these things. And see, I am sending upon you what my Father promised; so stay here in the city until you have been clothed with power from on high. "Then he led them out as far as Bethany, and, lifting up his hands, he blessed them. While he was blessing them, he withdrew from them and was carried up into heaven. And they worshiped him, and returned to Jerusalem with great joy; and they were continually in the temple blessing God.

This is the day when Christians rise
To study earnestly His Word,
Making commitment to their Lord,
To find Him holy, true and wise.

This is the day when Christians wait
At home, at work, in field and town:
Promise of power, not their own,
Will clothe them, bless them, recreate.

This is the day when Christians hear
His voice, who died for their fall,
Obey and listen: He sends all
To go, proclaim Him without fear.

This is the day when Christians laud,
In churches all around the earth,
God for the gift of life, the birth
Of Jesus, gone to be with God.

Words: Georg Retzlaff (b. 1946)
Music: *Herr, Jesu Christ, Dich zu uns wend'*, Johann Sebastian Bach, 1685-1750

88 88

Seventh Sunday of Easter

John 17:1-11

Jesus looked up to heaven and said, "Father, the hour has come; glorify your Son so that the Son may glorify you, since you have given him authority over all people, to give eternal life to all whom you have given him. And this is eternal life, that they may know you, the only true God, and Jesus Christ whom you have sent. I glorified you on earth by finishing the work that you gave me to do. So now, Father, glorify me in your own presence with the glory that I had in your presence before the world existed. "I have made your name known to those whom you gave me from the world. They were yours, and you gave them to me, and they have kept your word. Now they know that everything you have given me is from you; for the words that you gave to me I have given to them, and they have received them and know in truth that I came from you; and they have believed that you sent me. I am asking on their behalf; I am not asking on behalf of the world, but on behalf of those whom you gave me, because they are yours. All mine are yours, and yours are mine; and I have been glorified in them. And now I am no longer in the world, but they are in the world, and I am coming to you. Holy Father, protect them in your name that you have given me, so that they may be one, as we are one. "

Here is my hymn to God:
Thanksgiving for the Son,
Who was like Him and me,
And made us humans one.

My hearts breaks out with joy
Because of Him who gave
His life to make me see
That I am friend, not slave.

His prayers never end,
For unity and peace
Among the friends of God
And everyone who sees:

The Church of His is One,
United in one prayer:
That as He loved His God,
So we should love and care.

Words: Georg Retzlaff (b. 1946)
Music: *St. Cecilia*, Leighton G. Hayne, 1863
HPEC 1982, 613

6666

Day of Pentecost

John 20:19-23

When it was evening on that day, the first day of the week, and the doors of the house where the disciples had met were locked for fear of the Jews, Jesus came and stood among them and said, "Peace be with you." After he said this, he showed them his hands and his side. Then the disciples rejoiced when they saw the Lord. Jesus said to them again, "Peace be with you. As the Father has sent me, so I send you." When he had said this, he breathed on them and said to them, "Receive the Holy Spirit. If you forgive the sins of any, they are forgiven them; if you retain the sins of any, they are retained."

See what the Spirit does:
Fear of the enemies,
Banished for ever now,
Turns into lasting peace.

Feel, how the Spirit works:
Opening bolted doors,
Breathes into us new life,
On us His presence pours.

Sense, when the Spirit blows,
Far from the human heart,
Sins suffered, sins we did,
His Kingdom does impart.

Hear that the Spirit speaks,
Gives liberty to all:
Go out and share with joy
His everlasting call.

Words: Georg Retzlaff (b. 1946)
Music: *Quam dilecta*, Henry L. Jenner, 1861
HPEC 1982, 626

66 66

OR:

John 7:37-39

On the last day of the festival, the great day, while Jesus was standing there, he cried out, "Let anyone who is thirsty come to me, and let the one who believes in me drink. As the scripture has said, `Out of the believer's heart shall flow rivers of living water.'" Now he said this about the Spirit, which believers in him were to receive; for as yet there was no Spirit, because Jesus was not yet glorified.

Words: Georg Retzlaff (b. 1946)
Music: *Zoë*, Georg Retzlaff (b. 1946)

75 75

First Sunday after Pentecost: Trinity Sunday

Matthew 28:16-20

The eleven disciples went to Galilee, to the mountain to which Jesus had directed them. When they saw him, they worshiped him; but some doubted. And Jesus came and said to them, "All authority in heaven and on earth has been given to me. Go therefore and make disciples of all nations, baptizing them in the name of the Father and of the Son and of the Holy Spirit, and teaching them to obey everything that I have commanded you. And remember, I am with you always, to the end of the age."

I love Thee, Triune God,
My Father, part of me,
With soul and body, mind
I praise Thee: I am free.

I love Thee, Triune God,
For Jesus, part of me,
Who showed the Way to Life
Abundant: I am free.

I love Thee, Triune God,
Thy Spirit, part of me,
Fills every thought of mine,
And blesses: I am free.

I love Thee, Triune God,
For being mystery,
Not being any one
We fathom: Thou art free.

Words: Georg Retzlaff (b. 1946)
Music: *St. Cecilia*, Leighton George Hayne (1836-1883)
HPEC 1982, 613

66 66

Sunday Closest to May 11

Proper 1

Matthew 5:21-37

Jesus said, "You have heard that it was said to those of ancient times, 'You shall not murder'; and 'whoever murders shall be liable to judgment.' But I say to you that if you are angry with a brother or sister, you will be liable to judgment; and if you insult a brother or sister, you will be liable to the council; and if you say, 'You fool,' you will be liable to the hell of fire. So when you are offering your gift at the altar, if you remember that your brother or sister has something against you, leave your gift there before the altar and go; first be reconciled to your brother or sister, and then come and offer your gift. Come to terms quickly with your accuser while you are on the way to court with him, or your accuser may hand you over to the judge, and the judge to the guard, and you will be thrown into prison. Truly I tell you, you will never get out until you have paid the last penny. "You have heard that it was said, 'You shall not commit adultery.' But I say to you that everyone who looks at a woman with lust has already committed adultery with her in his heart. If your right eye causes you to sin, tear it out and throw it away; it is better for you to lose one of your members than for your whole body to be thrown into hell. And if your right hand causes you to sin, cut it off and throw it away; it is better for you to lose one of your members than for your whole body to go into hell. "It was also said, 'Whoever divorces his wife, let him give her a certificate of divorce.' But I say to you that anyone who divorces his wife, except on the ground of unchastity, causes her to commit adultery; and whoever marries a divorced woman commits adultery. "Again, you have heard that it was said to those of ancient times, 'You shall not swear falsely, but carry out the vows you have made to the Lord.' But I say to you, Do not swear at all, either by heaven, for it is the throne of God, or by the earth, for it is his footstool, or by Jerusalem, for it is the city of the great King. And do not swear by your head, for you cannot make one hair white or black. Let your word be 'Yes, Yes' or 'No, No'; anything more than this comes from the evil one.

It once was said, but is no more,
That law is law, and, set in stone,
Will judge the sinners, they alone
Must pay the price.

But then He spoke, our precious Lord,
Against the wisdom of the past,
And helped us not on sin to cast
Our prejudice.

We know now that it's not the deed
Which clouds the friendship with our God,
But rather thought, and nature prod
Us on to vice.

All praise to God who, through His Son,
Has opened up our eyes and mind,
To know humanity and find
His Grace suffice.

Words: Georg Retzlaff (b. 1946)
Music: *Gaza*, Traditional Jewish Melody, adapted 1919
HPEC 1940, 222

88 84

Sunday closest to May 18

Proper 2

Matthew 5:38-48

Jesus said, "You have heard that it was said, 'An eye for an eye and a tooth for a tooth.' But I say to you, Do not resist an evildoer. But if anyone strikes you on the right cheek, turn the other also; and if anyone wants to sue you and take your coat, give your cloak as well; and if anyone forces you to go one mile, go also the second mile. Give to everyone who begs from you, and do not refuse anyone who wants to borrow from you. "You have heard that it was said, 'You shall love your neighbor and hate your enemy.' But I say to you, Love your enemies and pray for those who persecute you, so that you may be children of your Father in heaven; for he makes his sun rise on the evil and on the good, and sends rain on the righteous and on the unrighteous. For if you love those who love you, what reward do you have? Do not even the tax collectors do the same? And if you greet only your brothers and sisters, what more are you doing than others? Do not even the Gentiles do the same? Be perfect, therefore, as your heavenly Father is perfect."

One Fath-er, one Lord, one call: Be per - fect, not con -
Learn love as it ne - ver was a - mong you lived or
A love that will go be - yond all boun - da - ries of
of those who will hate us now, to un - der - stand and
We of - fer all this to Him, who lived His life for

tent to com - pro - mise with - out end Good News
felt, not sen - ti - ment which can melt as snow
man, no en - mi - ty, e - vil can pre - vent
pray. a bles - sing for them to say, this is
us, when we were a - lone and lost, as our

pro - claimed to all.
is warmed and thaws.
us to be fond
our so - lemn vow.
e - ter - nal hymn.

Words: Georg Retzlaff (b. 1946)
Music: *St. Paulinus*, Georg Retzlaff (b. 1946)

76 76

Sunday Closest to May 25

Proper 3

Matthew 6:24-34

Jesus said, "No one can serve two masters; for a slave will either hate the one and love the other, or be devoted to the one and despise the other. You cannot serve God and wealth. "Therefore I tell you, do not worry about your life, what you will eat or what you will drink, or about your body, what you will wear. Is not life more than food, and the body more than clothing? Look at the birds of the air; they neither sow nor reap nor gather into barns, and yet your heavenly Father feeds them. Are you not of more value than they? And can any of you by worrying add a single hour to your span of life? And why do you worry about clothing? Consider the lilies of the field, how they grow; they neither toil nor spin, yet I tell you, even Solomon in all his glory was not clothed like one of these. But if God so clothes the grass of the field, which is alive today and tomorrow is thrown into the oven, will he not much more clothe you-- you of little faith? Therefore do not worry, saying, `What will we eat?' or `What will we drink?' or `What will we wear?' For it is the Gentiles who strive for all these things; and indeed your heavenly Father knows that you need all these things. But strive first for the kingdom of God and his righteousness, and all these things will be given to you as well. "So do not worry about tomorrow, for tomorrow will bring worries of its own. Today's trouble is enough for today."

The Kingdom He proclaimed is not above,
But now, within, and here,
And those who seek it find that all they need
Is theirs by Grace and Love.

If only we, like birds, would eat what God
Provides, with thankful hearts,
Content, and sharing all that grows around,
His blessings shed abroad!

If we, like lilies, dressed in beautiful
Attire to praise His Name,
Were frugal, unassuming, chaste and pure,
'Twere dignity for all.

If we could learn, like grass, to be of use,
Be kind to foot and eye,
Be humble, warm the souls of those grown cold,
The Kingdom would break loose.

Words: Georg Retzlaff (b. 1946)
Music: *St. Nicholas*, Clement C. Scholefield, 1870
HPEC 1940, 173

10 6 10 6

Sunday Closest to June 1

Proper 4

Matthew 7:21-29

Jesus said. "Not everyone who says to me, `Lord, Lord,' will enter the kingdom of heaven, but only the one who does the will of my Father in heaven. On that day many will say to me, `Lord, Lord, did we not prophesy in your name, and cast out demons in your name, and do many deeds of power in your name?' Then I will declare to them, `I never knew you; go away from me, you evildoers.' "Everyone then who hears these words of mine and acts on them will be like a wise man who built his house on rock. The rain fell, the floods came, and the winds blew and beat on that house, but it did not fall, because it had been founded on rock. And everyone who hears these words of mine and does not act on them will be like a foolish man who built his house on sand. The rain fell, and the floods came, and the winds blew and beat against that house, and it fell-- and great was its fall!" Now when Jesus had finished saying these things, the crowds were astounded at his teaching, for he taught them as one having authority, and not as their scribes.

O God, we pray Thee, strengthen trust,
Make it Thy sure abode,
A house on solid ground to withstand
Doubt and despair and lust.

The gentle rain we often ignore,
Soft'ning resolve and faith,
A drift away from prayer, from the church,
Love that we had before.

When catastrophic floods wash away
All we embraced til now,
Our goods, our health, our every desire,
Grant us another day.

Prepare us, Lord, for life's great storms,
When all things fall apart,
To look to Thee, the builder and guide
Who weary souls transforms.

Words: Georg Retzlaff (b. 1946)
Music: *Morning Song*, melody att. Elkanah Kelsay Dare (1782-1826) (alt)
HPEC 1982, 9

86 86

Sunday Closest to June 8

Proper 5

Matthew 9:9-13, 18-26

As Jesus was walking along, he saw a man called Matthew sitting at the tax booth; and he said to him, "Follow me." And he got up and followed him. And as he sat at dinner in the house, many tax collectors and sinners came and were sitting with him and his disciples. When the Pharisees saw this, they said to his disciples, "Why does your teacher eat with tax collectors and sinners?" But when he heard this, he said, "Those who are well have no need of a physician, but those who are sick. Go and learn what this means, `I desire mercy, not sacrifice.' For I have come to call not the righteous but sinners." While he was saying these things to them, suddenly a leader of the synagogue came in and knelt before him, saying, "My daughter has just died; but come and lay your hand on her, and she will live." And Jesus got up and followed him, with his disciples. Then suddenly a woman who had been suffering from hemorrhages for twelve years came up behind him and touched the fringe of his cloak, for she said to herself, "If I only touch his cloak, I will be made well." Jesus turned, and seeing her he said, "Take heart, daughter; your faith has made you well." And instantly the woman was made well. When Jesus came to the leader's house and saw the flute players and the crowd making a commotion, he said, "Go away; for the girl is not dead but sleeping." And they laughed at him. But when the crowd had been put outside, he went in and took her by the hand, and the girl got up. And the report of this spread throughout that district.

Neither the healthy, whole, nor happy
Will ever need His grace and touch.
Rather the struggling, sick, and sinful,
Whose burden is great, whose guilt is much.

They who have made their peace with Mammon,
Who love their lives more than their souls:
Sit at the feet of this physician,
Let Himgive purpose, end, and goals!

Illness and suffering: question Him,
Who tells us whether we must bear
Life's endless terror, or be freed
From shame, embarrassment, and fear.

Death, in its many forms, will haunt us,
When boy to man and girl to wife,
The living to the dead transform:
Lord, be with us and give us life.

Words: Georg Retzlaff (b. 1946)
Music: *St.Clement*, Clement C. Scholefield, 1874
HPEC 1982, 24

98 98

Sunday Closest to June 15

Proper 6

Matthew 9:35-10:8

Jesus went about all the cities and villages, teaching in their synagogues, and proclaiming the good news of the kingdom, and curing every disease and every sickness. When he saw the crowds, he had compassion for them, because they were harassed and helpless, like sheep without a shepherd. Then he said to his disciples, "The harvest is plentiful, but the laborers are few; therefore ask the Lord of the harvest to send out laborers into his harvest." Then Jesus summoned his twelve disciples and gave them authority over unclean spirits, to cast them out, and to cure every disease and every sickness. These are the names of the twelve apostles: first, Simon, also known as Peter, and his brother Andrew; James son of Zebedee, and his brother John; Philip and Bartholomew; Thomas and Matthew the tax collector; James son of Alphaeus, and Thaddaeus; Simon the Cananaean, and Judas Iscariot, the one who betrayed him. These twelve Jesus sent out with the following instructions: "Go nowhere among the Gentiles, and enter no town of the Samaritans, but go rather to the lost sheep of the house of Israel. As you go, proclaim the good news, 'The kingdom of heaven has come near.' Cure the sick, raise the dead, cleanse the lepers, cast out demons. You received without payment; give without payment.

Twelve were called at first, today
Many more are gathered here,
Praying for the Lord to send
Workers out, His prayer to hear.

Jesus prays and gives the charge:
What you pray for you should do,
As you've witnessed ministry,
Imitate, do likewise, go.

Work your miracles of trust
In the power of faith and love,
Cure the sick and raise the dead,
Cleanse the lepers, rise above.

Look inside you, go not far,
Try not to redeem the world,
Kingdom's bliss begins in you,
Where the gospel is unfurled.

Twelve are called today, not more,
Willing to devote their lives,
To the harvest of all time,
For the blessing which He gives.

Words: Georg Retzlaff (b. 1946)
Music: *Buckland*, Leighton G. Hayne, 1863
HPEC 1940, 428

77 77

Sunday closest to June 22

Proper 7

Matthew 10:24-39

Jesus said to the twelve disciples, "A disciple is not above the teacher, nor a slave above the master; it is enough for the disciple to be like the teacher, and the slave like the master. If they have called the master of the house Beelzebul, how much more will they malign those of his household! "So have no fear of them; for nothing is covered up that will not be uncovered, and nothing secret that will not become known. What I say to you in the dark, tell in the light; and what you hear whispered, proclaim from the housetops. Do not fear those who kill the body but cannot kill the soul; rather fear him who can destroy both soul and body in hell. Are not two sparrows sold for a penny? Yet not one of them will fall to the ground apart from your Father. And even the hairs of your head are all counted. So do not be afraid; you are of more value than many sparrows. "Everyone therefore who acknowledges me before others, I also will acknowledge before my Father in heaven; but whoever denies me before others, I also will deny before my Father in heaven. "Do not think that I have come to bring peace to the earth; I have not come to bring peace, but a sword. "For I have come to set a man against his father, and a daughter against her mother, and a daughter-in-law against her mother-in-law; and one's foes will be members of one's own household. "Whoever loves father or mother more than me is not worthy of me; and whoever loves son or daughter more than me is not worthy of me; and whoever does not take up the cross and follow me is not worthy of me. Those who find their life will lose it, and those who lose their life for my sake will find it."

O Christians, think before you
Decide to follow Him,
Remember now His solemn words,
And search for truth within.

They who would call upon His Name,
Are learners all their lives,
And servants of a needy world
Which them of pride deprives.

Acknowledge Him before all men,
Speak peace when there is war,
Then you will find the sword is drawn
Between those near and far.

The love for Himwill cost you
The comforts you have known,
But you who dare to lose your lives
Will gain of life the crown.

Words: Georg Retzlaff (b. 1946)
Music: *Wohl heute noch und morgen*, Silesian Folk Tune, c. 1818

86 86

Sunday closest to June 29

Proper 8

Matthew 10:40-42

Jesus said, "Whoever welcomes you welcomes me, and whoever welcomes me welcomes the one who sent me. Whoever welcomes a prophet in the name of a prophet will receive a prophet's reward; and whoever welcomes a righteous person in the name of a righteous person will receive the reward of the righteous; and whoever gives even a cup of cold water to one of these little ones in the name of a disciple-- truly I tell you, none of these will lose their reward."

For far too long we've turned to stars,
And looked to prophecy divine,
An ancient, uttering wisdom
For his time, not for ours.

We searched for God in righteousness,
With law to punish and reward
The race of humans eager
To bow and seek redress.

We were in error when we sought
The praise of men by charity,
To gain from God a favor
For all the good we wrought.

Our Lord invites us, shows the way
To greater joy and benefit:
Let others see Him in us,
And to the Father pray.

To whom be praise eternally,
Our God who lives beyond the world,
Who, through His Son and Spirit,
Has set His children free.

Words: Georg Retzlaff (b. 1946)
Music: *Es geht eine dunkle Wolke*, Pater J. Werlin, 1646

88 76

Sunday closest to July 6

Proper 9

Matthew 11:16-19, 25-30

Jesus said to the crowd, "To what will I compare this generation? It is like children sitting in the marketplaces and calling to one another, 'We played the flute for you, and you did not dance; we wailed, and you did not mourn.' For John came neither eating nor drinking, and they say, 'He has a demon'; the Son of Man came eating and drinking, and they say, 'Look, a glutton and a drunkard, a friend of tax collectors and sinners!' Yet wisdom is vindicated by her deeds." At that time Jesus said, "I thank you, Father, Lord of heaven and earth, because you have hidden these things from the wise and the intelligent and have revealed them to infants; yes, Father, for such was your gracious will. All things have been handed over to me by my Father; and no one knows the Son except the Father, and no one knows the Father except the Son and anyone to whom the Son chooses to reveal him. "Come to me, all you that are weary and are carrying heavy burdens, and I will give you rest. Take my yoke upon you, and learn from me; for I am gentle and humble in heart, and you will find rest for your souls. For my yoke is easy, and my burden is light."

Come to me and bring
Me all your suffering,
All that hurts and pains,
Disappointments, sins.
My yoke is easy, light
Relieves you of your plight.

Place your foolish thought
About what God has wrought,
What He wants to do
At my feet, renew
Your thinking of His plan,
Believe the Son of Man!

Never flute nor dance,
Neither the mind's expanse
Can bestow my peace,
Make confusion ease,
But yearning, when my word
By humble ears is heard.

Words: Georg Retzlaff (b. 1946)
Music: *Du mein einzig Licht*, Heinrich Albert (1604-1651)
56 55 66

Sunday closest to July 13

Proper 10

Matthew 13:1-9,18-23

Jesus went out of the house and sat beside the sea. Such great crowds gathered around him that he got into a boat and sat there, while the whole crowd stood on the beach. And he told them many things in parables, saying: "Listen! A sower went out to sow. And as he sowed, some seeds fell on the path, and the birds came and ate them up. Other seeds fell on rocky ground, where they did not have much soil, and they sprang up quickly, since they had no depth of soil. But when the sun rose, they were scorched; and since they had no root, they withered away. Other seeds fell among thorns, and the thorns grew up and choked them. Other seeds fell on good soil and brought forth grain, some a hundredfold, some sixty, some thirty. Let anyone with ears listen!" "Hear then the parable of the sower. When anyone hears the word of the kingdom and does not understand it, the evil one comes and snatches away what is sown in the heart; this is what was sown on the path. As for what was sown on rocky ground, this is the one who hears the word and immediately receives it with joy; yet such a person has no root, but endures only for a while, and when trouble or persecution arises on account of the word, that person immediately falls away. As for what was sown among thorns, this is the one who hears the word, but the cares of the world and the lure of wealth choke the word, and it yields nothing. But as for what was sown on good soil, this is the one who hears the word and understands it, who indeed bears fruit and yields, in one case a hundredfold, in another sixty, and in another thirty."

Go, scatter, do not mind the work, just throw the seed,
Look not at barren soil or hungry birds that feed,
Waste not your time in fretting over
Those whose ears are deaf or closed,
Be steadfast, be a sower!

Be not discouraged nor impatient when you teach,
In school, or home, in working place, at church you preach!
Here is your place for you to flourish,
Share the Gospel and your faith,
Give food for thought, and nourish.

Remember that your Father's kindness sheltered you
In times of ignorance, rebellion, when your due
Should have been punishment and sorrow,
But He scattered, waited, hoped
That there would be tomorrow.

Words: Georg Retzlaff (b. 1946)
Music: *All mein Gedanken*, Lochheimer Liederbuch (Nürnberg, 1452-1460)

12 12 9 77

Sunday closest to July 20

Proper 11

Matthew 13:24-30,36-43

Jesus put before the crowd another parable: "The kingdom of heaven may be compared to someone who sowed good seed in his field; but while everybody was asleep, an enemy came and sowed weeds among the wheat, and then went away. So when the plants came up and bore grain, then the weeds appeared as well. And the slaves of the householder came and said to him, 'Master, did you not sow good seed in your field? Where, then, did these weeds come from?' He answered, 'An enemy has done this.' The slaves said to him, 'Then do you want us to go and gather them?' But he replied, 'No; for in gathering the weeds you would uproot the wheat along with them. Let both of them grow together until the harvest; and at harvest time I will tell the reapers, Collect the weeds first and bind them in bundles to be burned, but gather the wheat into my barn.'" Then he left the crowds and went into the house. And his disciples approached him, saying, "Explain to us the parable of the weeds of the field." He answered, "The one who sows the good seed is the Son of Man; the field is the world, and the good seed are the children of the kingdom; the weeds are the children of the evil one, and the enemy who sowed them is the devil; the harvest is the end of the age, and the reapers are angels. Just as the weeds are collected and burned up with fire, so will it be at the end of the age. The Son of Man will send his angels, and they will collect out of his kingdom all causes of sin and all evildoers, and they will throw them into the furnace of fire, where there will be weeping and gnashing of teeth. Then the righteous will shine like the sun in the kingdom of their Father. Let anyone with ears listen!"

When God begins to bless a soul,
With great awakening, deep within,
Be ready, field, for sowing.

When sun and soil and water give
All that a fledgling faith will need,
Stretch roots, stems, blossoms growing.

There will be time when one regrets,
And wishes for the fallow past,
When arid winds were blowing.

Because with wheat the weeds appear,
And soil the beauty of the field,
So wanted, without knowing.

God gives all growth, and He does clear
What's not of Him, and He, by grace,
His Kingdom is bestowing.

Words: Georg Retzlaff (b. 1946)
Music: *Gesegn dich Laub*, 16th century, German

887

Sunday closest to July 27

Proper 12

Matthew 13:31-33,44-52

Jesus put before the crowds another parable: "The kingdom of heaven is like a mustard seed that someone took and sowed in his field; it is the smallest of all the seeds, but when it has grown it is the greatest of shrubs and becomes a tree, so that the birds of the air come and make nests in its branches."He told them another parable: "The kingdom of heaven is like yeast that a woman took and mixed in with three measures of flour until all of it was leavened.""The kingdom of heaven is like treasure hidden in a field, which someone found and hid; then in his joy he goes and sells all that he has and buys that field. "Again, the kingdom of heaven is like a merchant in search of fine pearls; on finding one pearl of great value, he went and sold all that he had and bought it. "Again, the kingdom of heaven is like a net that was thrown into the sea and caught fish of every kind; when it was full, they drew it ashore, sat down, and put the good into baskets but threw out the bad. So it will be at the end of the age. The angels will come out and separate the evil from the righteous and throw them into the furnace of fire, where there will be weeping and gnashing of teeth. "Have you understood all this?" They answered, "Yes." And he said to them, "Therefore every scribe who has been trained for the kingdom of heaven is like the master of a household who brings out of his treasure what is new and what is old."

The Master speaks, brings treasures forth,
As small as mustard seeds they are.
They need no work but patience, yet
The Kingdom's yeast requires more:
Both work and wait,
Both work and wait.

He offers us abundant life,
Directs our souls and lazy eyes
To buried, precious things below,
Where truth is waiting, of great prize,
To make us grow,
To make us grow.

At His command we cast our nets,
Into the sea of life and catch
A plethora of blessings, though
To keep, we rule, or to dispatch,
God's glory show,
God's glory show.

Words: Georg Retzlaff (b. 1946)
Music: *Ich fahr' dahin*, Lochheimer Liederbuch, 1452

88 88 44

Sunday Closest to August 3

Proper 13

Matthew 14:13-21

Jesus withdrew in a boat to a deserted place by himself. But when the crowds heard it, they followed him on foot from the towns. When he went ashore, he saw a great crowd; and he had compassion for them and cured their sick. When it was evening, the disciples came to him and said, "This is a deserted place, and the hour is now late; send the crowds away so that they may go into the villages and buy food for themselves." Jesus said to them, "They need not go away; you give them something to eat." They replied, "We have nothing here but five loaves and two fish." And he said, "Bring them here to me." Then he ordered the crowds to sit down on the grass. Taking the five loaves and the two fish, he looked up to heaven, and blessed and broke the loaves, and gave them to the disciples, and the disciples gave them to the crowds. And all ate and were filled; and they took up what was left over of the broken pieces, twelve baskets full. And those who ate were about five thousand men, besides women and children.

You who would wonders and miracles see
Come by yourselves to a desolate place.
Learn not to do or to work but to be
Sheltered in God's all-encompassing grace.
Take your possessions and offer them all,
Heeding your Lord's invitation and call.

Look all around you, sit on the green ground,
Open your hearts to your neighbors in love;
Reach out in friendship to him whom you found
Searching, as you have, for heaven above.
Open your hands and receive blessed bread,
Be in your bodies and in your souls fed.

Gather the fragments, give glory to God,
Make this a wonder, be still and be awed.
Learn how a little can satisfy man,
How to give thanks to the God of all life;
That by our sharing a miracle can
Happen which will deliver us from strife.

Words: Georg Retzlaff (b. 1946)
Music: *Ännchen von Tharau*, W.F. Silcher (1789-1860)

10 10 10 10 10 10

Sunday closest to August 10

Proper 14

Matthew 14:22-33

Jesus made the disciples get into the boat and go on ahead to the other side, while he dismissed the crowds. And after he had dismissed the crowds, he went up the mountain by himself to pray. When evening came, he was there alone, but by this time the boat, battered by the waves, was far from the land, for the wind was against them. And early in the morning he came walking toward them on the sea. But when the disciples saw him walking on the sea, they were terrified, saying, "It is a ghost!" And they cried out in fear. But immediately Jesus spoke to them and said, "Take heart, it is I; do not be afraid." Peter answered him, "Lord, if it is you, command me to come to you on the water." He said, "Come." So Peter got out of the boat, started walking on the water, and came toward Jesus. But when he noticed the strong wind, he became frightened, and beginning to sink, he cried out, "Lord, save me!" Jesus immediately reached out his hand and caught him, saying to him, "You of little faith, why did you doubt?" When they got into the boat, the wind ceased. And those in the boat worshiped him, saying, "Truly you are the Son of God."

O Thou who art in storm and sea
Who guidest us to shore,
Be with us, come to us and free
Us from our lives before
We heard your voice: Take heart!

O Thou who hoverest above
The waters and didst give,
Like in the ancient days the dove,
To all creation life,
Oh speak now: It is I!

Lift from us fear and dread of doom,
Give us a heart of trust,
Help us to see Thee and give room
To deeper faith which must
Say boldly: Have no fear!

And then, we humbly pray Thee, take
Our boat to where Thou wilt;
If only we, for Thy Name's sake,
And with Thy presence filled,
Let Thou be our guide!

Words: Georg Retzlaff (b. 1946)
Music: *Siroë,* Georg Friedrich Händel (1685-1759)
HPEC 1982, 546

86 866

Sunday closest to August 17

Proper 15

Matthew 15: (10-20), 21-28

Jesus called the crowd to him and said to them, "Listen and understand: it is not what goes into the mouth that defiles a person, but it is what comes out of the mouth that defiles." Then the disciples approached and said to him, "Do you know that the Pharisees took offense when they heard what you said?" He answered, "Every plant that my heavenly Father has not planted will be uprooted. Let them alone; they are blind guides of the blind. And if one blind person guides another, both will fall into a pit." But Peter said to him, "Explain this parable to us." Then he said, "Are you also still without understanding? Do you not see that whatever goes into the mouth enters the stomach, and goes out into the sewer? But what comes out of the mouth proceeds from the heart, and this is what defiles. For out of the heart come evil intentions, murder, adultery, fornication, theft, false witness, slander. These are what defile a person, but to eat with unwashed hands does not defile."] Jesus left Gennesaret and went away to the district of Tyre and Sidon. Just then a Canaanite woman from that region came out and started shouting, "Have mercy on me, Lord, Son of David; my daughter is tormented by a demon." But he did not answer her at all. And his disciples came and urged him, saying, "Send her away, for she keeps shouting after us." He answered, "I was sent only to the lost sheep of the house of Israel." But she came and knelt before him, saying, "Lord, help me." He answered, "It is not fair to take the children's food and throw it to the dogs." She said, "Yes, Lord, yet even the dogs eat the crumbs that fall from their masters' table." Then Jesus answered her, "Woman, great is your faith! Let it be done for you as you wish." And her daughter was healed instantly.

It is in times of great distress,
When earthly burdens trouble
That human love exhausts itself,
It needs to rest
In Thee, God, and love double.

Not sentiment nor flutt'ring heart,
But mercy, deep and sweeping,
Going beyond what he has known,
Makes man impart
Comfort and end of weeping.

She was not worthy, nor are we,
To gather crumbs for eating,
But Thou alone art the same Lord
Whose property
Is always to have mercy.

Words: Georg Retzlaff (b. 1946)
Music: *Ich weiss ein lieblich Engelspiel*, Heinrich von Laufenberg (1390-1458)

87 8 4 7

Sunday closest to August 24

Proper 16

Matthew 16:13-20

When Jesus came into the district of Caesarea Philippi, he asked his disciples, "Who do people say that the Son of Man is?" And they said, "Some say John the Baptist, but others Elijah, and still others Jeremiah or one of the prophets." He said to them, "But who do you say that I am?" Simon Peter answered, "You are the Messiah, the Son of the living God." And Jesus answered him, "Blessed are you, Simon son of Jonah! For flesh and blood has not revealed this to you, but my Father in heaven. And I tell you, you are Peter, and on this rock I will build my church, and the gates of Hades will not prevail against it. I will give you the keys of the kingdom of heaven, and whatever you bind on earth will be bound in heaven, and whatever you loose on earth will be loosed in heaven." Then he sternly ordered the disciples not to tell anyone that he was the Messiah.

Who do we say He is?
To whom should we compare
This Lord, this Friend, and Lover
Of lost and sinful nature?
A man unlike another,
From God and from the future.

Who do we say He is?
An image of what was
Prophetic past, Elijah,
The Baptist's pale remembrance,
A second Jeremiah,
God's messenger of vengeance?

Who do we say He is?
Abandon all you've learned,
And greet the new, life-giving,
For ever blessed Savior,
Who, all of us inviting,
Bestows the keys to heaven's door.

Words: Georg Retzlaff (b. 1946)
Music: *Die liebe Maienzeit*, Melchior Franck, 1611

667777

Sunday closest to August 31

Proper 17

Matthew 16:21-28

Jesus began to show his disciples that he must go to Jerusalem and undergo great suffering at the hands of the elders and chief priests and scribes, and be killed, and on the third day be raised. And Peter took him aside and began to rebuke him, saying, "God forbid it, Lord! This must never happen to you." But he turned and said to Peter, "Get behind me, Satan! You are a stumbling block to me; for you are setting your mind not on divine things but on human things." Then Jesus told his disciples, "If any want to become my followers, let them deny themselves and take up their cross and follow me. For those who want to save their life will lose it, and those who lose their life for my sake will find it. For what will it profit them if they gain the whole world but forfeit their life? Or what will they give in return for their life? "For the Son of Man is to come with his angels in the glory of his Father, and then he will repay everyone for what has been done. Truly I tell you, there are some standing here who will not taste death before they see the Son of Man coming in his kingdom."

All creatures love the Lord on high,
They send their prayers with a sigh,
In hope of blessings for their lives:
For their own families, husbands, wives.

Yet not what man can get from God
Will ever change the way he trod,
But what he offers, Self and soul,
Will redefine his life and his goal.

Deny your Self, take up the cross,
And follow Him who counts as dross
Temerity and shallowness,
Be His disciples and let Him bless.

Words: Georg Retzlaff (b. 1946)
Music: *Es steht ein Lind*, Souterliedekens, 1540

8889

Sunday closest to September 7

Proper 18

Matthew 18:15-20

Jesus said, "If another member of the church sins against you, go and point out the fault when the two of you are alone. If the member listens to you, you have regained that one. But if you are not listened to, take one or two others along with you, so that every word may be confirmed by the evidence of two or three witnesses. If the member refuses to listen to them, tell it to the church; and if the offender refuses to listen even to the church, let such a one be to you as a Gentile and a tax collector. Truly I tell you, whatever you bind on earth will be bound in heaven, and whatever you loose on earth will be loosed in heaven. Again, truly I tell you, if two of you agree on earth about anything you ask, it will be done for you by my Father in heaven. For where two or three are gathered in my name, I am there among them."

We praise you, God, for Mother Church,
Where sinners gather and are blessed,
Not for their sin, but for their search
After new life, in earnest zest.

Here we will listen and correct
Our faulty ways, our haughtiness,
Submit to discipline, expect
Redeeming love and tenderness.

This is the place for two or three,
not many hundreds of a crowd,
This is the moment you can see
His Presence promised and avowed.

Words: Georg Retzlaff (b. 1946)
Music: *Die helle Sonn*, Melchior Vulpius, 1609

88 88

Sunday closest to September 14

Proper 19

Matthew 18:21-35

Peter came and said to Jesus, "Lord, if another member of the church sins against me, how often should I forgive? As many as seven times?" Jesus said to him, "Not seven times, but, I tell you, seventy-seven times. "For this reason the kingdom of heaven may be compared to a king who wished to settle accounts with his slaves. When he began the reckoning, one who owed him ten thousand talents was brought to him; and, as he could not pay, his lord ordered him to be sold, together with his wife and children and all his possessions, and payment to be made. So the slave fell on his knees before him, saying, 'Have patience with me, and I will pay you everything.' And out of pity for him, the lord of that slave released him and forgave him the debt. But that same slave, as he went out, came upon one of his fellow slaves who owed him a hundred denarii; and seizing him by the throat, he said, 'Pay what you owe.' Then his fellow slave fell down and pleaded with him, 'Have patience with me, and I will pay you.' But he refused; then he went and threw him into prison until he would pay the debt. When his fellow slaves saw what had happened, they were greatly distressed, and they went and reported to their lord all that had taken place. Then his lord summoned him and said to him, 'You wicked slave! I forgave you all that debt because you pleaded with me. Should you not have had mercy on your fellow slave, as I had mercy on you?' And in anger his lord handed him over to be tortured until he would pay his entire debt. So my heavenly Father will also do to every one of you, if you do not forgive your brother or sister from your heart."

God is grace, and endless pardon
Is His gift to needy souls
:When they come:
To His throne, and He paroles.

God cannot but spread His mantle
Of forgiveness over all
:Those who have failed:
Understanding Jesus' call.

God will bless them who remember
How their debt was washed away
:In the blood:
Of the Lamb who helps us say:

No, not seven times but always
Shall I offer the healing hand,
:Doing the work:
All according to His command.

Words: Georg Retzlaff (b. 1946)
Music: *Stehn zwei Stern*, German Traditional

88 44 8

Sunday closest to September 21

Proper 20

Matthew 20:1-16

Jesus said, "The kingdom of heaven is like a landowner who went out early in the morning to hire laborers for his vineyard. After agreeing with the laborers for the usual daily wage, he sent them into his vineyard. When he went out about nine o'clock, he saw others standing idle in the marketplace; and he said to them, 'You also go into the vineyard, and I will pay you whatever is right.' So they went. When he went out again about noon and about three o'clock, he did the same. And about five o'clock he went out and found others standing around; and he said to them, 'Why are you standing here idle all day?' They said to him, 'Because no one has hired us.' He said to them, 'You also go into the vineyard.' When evening came, the owner of the vineyard said to his manager, 'Call the laborers and give them their pay, beginning with the last and then going to the first.' When those hired about five o'clock came, each of them received the usual daily wage. Now when the first came, they thought they would receive more; but each of them also received the usual daily wage. And when they received it, they grumbled against the landowner, saying, 'These last worked only one hour, and you have made them equal to us who have borne the burden of the day and the scorching heat.' But he replied to one of them, 'Friend, I am doing you no wrong; did you not agree with me for the usual daily wage? Take what belongs to you and go; I choose to give to this last the same as I give to you. Am I not allowed to do what I choose with what belongs to me? Or are you envious because I am generous?' So the last will be first, and the first will be last."

We thank you, God, for workplace,
Employment and our wage,
We praise you that our labors
Are blessèd by your grace.
Through what we do we praise you,
Express the gifts you gave.
There is no curse on humans
Who till, create, and do.

Give us, o Lord, true feelings
For those who idly stand
In daily scorching markets,
And wait for him who brings
A Kingdom in which husband ,
Both children, wife, and kin,
Can share the loaves of justice,
And praise your mighty hand.

Words: Georg Retzlaff (b. 1946)
Music: *Kein Hälmlein wächst auf Erden*, Emil Brachvogel (1824-1878)

76 76 76 76

Sunday closest to September 28

Proper 21

Matthew 21:23-32

When Jesus entered the temple, the chief priests and the elders of the people came to him as he was teaching, and said, "By what authority are you doing these things, and who gave you this authority?" Jesus said to them, "I will also ask you one question; if you tell me the answer, then I will also tell you by what authority I do these things. Did the baptism of John come from heaven, or was it of human origin?" And they argued with one another, "If we say, `From heaven,' he will say to us, `Why then did you not believe him?' But if we say, `Of human origin,' we are afraid of the crowd; for all regard John as a prophet." So they answered Jesus, "We do not know." And he said to them, "Neither will I tell you by what authority I am doing these things. "What do you think? A man had two sons; he went to the first and said, `Son, go and work in the vineyard today.' He answered, `I will not'; but later he changed his mind and went. The father went to the second and said the same; and he answered, `I go, sir'; but he did not go. Which of the two did the will of his father?" They said, "The first." Jesus said to them, "Truly I tell you, the tax collectors and the prostitutes are going into the kingdom of God ahead of you. For John came to you in the way of righteousness and you did not believe him, but the tax collectors and the prostitutes believed him; and even after you saw it, you did not change your minds and believe him."

To words we listen, words we speak,
A cloud of chatter and of sounds
Our shallow, empty lives surrounds,
Obscures the holy truth we seek.

O Lord, teach us to say a Yes,
From heart to heart, without conceit
Or reservation. It is meet
And right with deeds our words to bless.

Have mercy, Father, on our No
Of anger, ignorance, or doubt,
What, in rebellion, we throughout
Our lives have done, although we know

That you will greet the wayward child,
The one who struggles, wrestles, fights
The gospel grace, until his sights
Are set on truth and mercy mild.

Words: Georg Retzlaff (b. 1946)
Music: *Wo Gott zum Haus nicht gibt sein Gunst*, Hans Leo Haßler, 1610

88 88

Sunday closest to October 5

Proper 22

Matthew 21:33-46

Jesus said, "Listen to another parable. There was a landowner who planted a vineyard, put a fence around it, dug a wine press in it, and built a watchtower. Then he leased it to tenants and went to another country. When the harvest time had come, he sent his slaves to the tenants to collect his produce. But the tenants seized his slaves and beat one, killed another, and stoned another. Again he sent other slaves, more than the first; and they treated them in the same way. Finally he sent his son to them, saying, 'They will respect my son.' But when the tenants saw the son, they said to themselves, 'This is the heir; come, let us kill him and get his inheritance.' So they seized him, threw him out of the vineyard, and killed him. Now when the owner of the vineyard comes, what will he do to those tenants?" They said to him, "He will put those wretches to a miserable death, and lease the vineyard to other tenants who will give him the produce at the harvest time." Jesus said to them, "Have you never read in the scriptures:'The stone that the builders rejected has become the cornerstone; this was the Lord's doing, and it is amazing in our eyes'? Therefore I tell you, the kingdom of God will be taken away from you and given to a people that produces the fruits of the kingdom. The one who falls on this stone will be broken to pieces; and it will crush anyone on whom it falls."When the chief priests and the Pharisees heard his parables, they realized that he was speaking about them. They wanted to arrest him, but they feared the crowds, because they regarded him as a prophet.

This is amazing in our eyes
That God has never wavered,
That He has planted, watered, dug
In restive souls a vineyard
To grow His fruit and labored

To bring His peace to sinful men
Who seek their own, who care not
About His blessings, undeserved,
Refuse to thank, as they aught,
The One who by His blood bought

A new world, filled with grateful hearts
Who, though they once rejected
Their Savior, now with joyful noise
Will bear the fruit expected
Of those by grace elected.

Words: Georg Retzlaff (b. 1946)
Music: *Verleih uns Frieden gnädiglich*, Johann Chr. G. Stade, ed. 1830

87 877

Sunday closest to October 12

Proper 23

Matthew 22:1-14

Once more Jesus spoke to the people in parables, saying: "The kingdom of heaven may be compared to a king who gave a wedding banquet for his son. He sent his slaves to call those who had been invited to the wedding banquet, but they would not come. Again he sent other slaves, saying, 'Tell those who have been invited: Look, I have prepared my dinner, my oxen and my fat calves have been slaughtered, and everything is ready; come to the wedding banquet.' But they made light of it and went away, one to his farm, another to his business, while the rest seized his slaves, mistreated them, and killed them. The king was enraged. He sent his troops, destroyed those murderers, and burned their city. Then he said to his slaves, 'The wedding is ready, but those invited were not worthy. Go therefore into the main streets, and invite everyone you find to the wedding banquet.' Those slaves went out into the streets and gathered all whom they found, both good and bad; so the wedding hall was filled with guests. "But when the king came in to see the guests, he noticed a man there who was not wearing a wedding robe, and he said to him, 'Friend, how did you get in here without a wedding robe?' And he was speechless. Then the king said to the attendants, 'Bind him hand and foot, and throw him into the outer darkness, where there will be weeping and gnashing of teeth.' For many are called, but few are chosen."

Our God forgives the sinners
Whose ears are stopped and dull,
Who cannot, will not listen
To His most gracious call:
Come to the banquet!

By manifold excuses
They hide from God, or fight
Against the loving presence
Of Him who does invite:
Come to the banquet!

God's violence and anger
Is not from Him but us,
Resenting His wide mercy
Who evermore speaks thus:
Come to the banquet!

Thanksgiving to the Father,
He blessed us with a Son
Who, through the Spirit, offers
To make our sin His own:
Come to the banquet!

Words: Georg Retzlaff (b. 1946)
Music: *Und unser lieben Frauen*, Nikolaus Beuttner's Gesangbuch, 1602

76765

Sunday closest to October 19

Proper 24

Matthew 22:15-22

The Pharisees went and plotted to entrap Jesus in what he said. So they sent their disciples to him, along with the Herodians, saying, "Teacher, we know that you are sincere, and teach the way of God in accordance with truth, and show deference to no one; for you do not regard people with partiality. Tell us, then, what you think. Is it lawful to pay taxes to the emperor, or not?" But Jesus, aware of their malice, said, "Why are you putting me to the test, you hypocrites? Show me the coin used for the tax." And they brought him a denarius. Then he said to them, "Whose head is this, and whose title?" They answered, "The emperor's." Then he said to them, "Give therefore to the emperor the things that are the emperor's, and to God the things that are God's." When they heard this, they were amazed; and they left him and went away.

Amid conflicting loyalties
The Christian treads his path,
There are his neighbors, countrymen,
And God, His love or wrath
To gain or circumvent.

When things that rightfully are God's
Are given back to Him,
Ask, Christian, what is in your hand?
A coin, an image, dim,
Of those who rule the land.

Allegiance is to God alone:
Proclaim this boldly now!
And pray the mighty of our time
Will know their place and bow
Their heads, from mountains climb.

A world according to God's will
Sees Christians challenge power,
Disciples, holding high their coin,
Refuse to fear and cower:
Now God and world rejoin.

Words: Georg Retzlaff (b. 1946)
Music: *Lobt Gott, Ihr Christen, allzugleich*, Nikolaus Hermann (1480-1561); harm.
Johann S. Bach (1685-1750)

86 866

Sunday closest to October 26

Proper 25

Matthew 22:34-46

When the Pharisees heard that Jesus had silenced the Sadducees, they gathered together, and one of them, a lawyer, asked him a question to test him. "Teacher, which commandment in the law is the greatest?" He said to him, "'You shall love the Lord your God with all your heart, and with all your soul, and with all your mind.' This is the greatest and first commandment. And a second is like it: 'You shall love your neighbor as yourself.' On these two commandments hang all the law and the prophets."Now while the Pharisees were gathered together, Jesus asked them this question: "What do you think of the Messiah? Whose son is he?" They said to him, "The son of David." He said to them, "How is it then that David by the Spirit calls him Lord, saying,'The Lord said to my Lord, "Sit at my right hand, until I put your enemies under your feet"'? If David thus calls him Lord, how can he be his son?" No one was able to give him an answer, nor from that day did anyone dare to ask him any more questions.

God's Holy One in wisdom
Came freedom us to bring,
To tear the veil of boredom
Off stale religion, sing
A new song to the King.

The pious and the mighty,
Who in their learning bask,
Have questions, dull and flighty,
They know not how to ask,
They know not what their task.

Hear now, be still and quiet:
In Jesus, Law is done,
He Goes beyond the Prophets,
Messiahs, David's son,
He is above, the One.

Words: Georg Retzlaff (b. 1946)
Music: *Mit Lust tät ich ausreiten*, after Johann Ott, 1534

76 766

Sunday closest to November 2

Proper 26

Matthew 23:1-12

Jesus said to the crowds and to his disciples, "The scribes and the Pharisees sit on Moses' seat; therefore, do whatever they teach you and follow it; but do not do as they do, for they do not practice what they teach. They tie up heavy burdens, hard to bear, and lay them on the shoulders of others; but they themselves are unwilling to lift a finger to move them. They do all their deeds to be seen by others; for they make their phylacteries broad and their fringes long. They love to have the place of honor at banquets and the best seats in the synagogues, and to be greeted with respect in the marketplaces, and to have people call them rabbi. But you are not to be called rabbi, for you have one teacher, and you are all students. And call no one your father on earth, for you have one Father-- the one in heaven. Nor are you to be called instructors, for you have one instructor, the Messiah. The greatest among you will be your servant. All who exalt themselves will be humbled, and all who humble themselves will be exalted."

The Father's Word is holy,
Touching human hearts.
It's truth depends not on its preacher,
What he may practice daily,
But blessing it imparts

On people who are humble,
Love no dress nor show,
Who are at one with Him who taught them.
And even if they stumble,
Will not His grace forgo.

They shun the seats of honor,
Know their place in life,
Resent the empty praise of titles,
Embrace and love the other
Until His days arrive.

Words: Georg Retzlaff (b. 1946)
Music: *Drei Laub auf einer Linden*, Traditional, c. 1540

75 9 76

Sunday closest to November 9

Proper 27

Matthew 25:1-13

Jesus said, "Then the kingdom of heaven will be like this. Ten bridesmaids took their lamps and went to meet the bridegroom. Five of them were foolish, and five were wise. When the foolish took their lamps, they took no oil with them; but the wise took flasks of oil with their lamps. As the bridegroom was delayed, all of them became drowsy and slept. But at midnight there was a shout, `Look! Here is the bridegroom! Come out to meet him.' Then all those bridesmaids got up and trimmed their lamps. The foolish said to the wise, `Give us some of your oil, for our lamps are going out.' But the wise replied, `No! there will not be enough for you and for us; you had better go to the dealers and buy some for yourselves.' And while they went to buy it, the bridegroom came, and those who were ready went with him into the wedding banquet; and the door was shut. Later the other bridesmaids came also, saying, `Lord, lord, open to us.' But he replied, `Truly I tell you, I do not know you.' Keep awake therefore, for you know neither the day nor the hour."

Not sin, o God, nor righteousness,
Not wrong or holiness,
But wisdom you look for, a lamp shining brightly,
A new way of thinking about heaven rightly,
Ending all foolishness.

Be wise, o friend, soar on your wings,
Don't rush in Kingdom things.
The price of a life-long commitment consider,
The time you have left, which is gone, you must ponder,
Purchase the peace He brings.

We are together in God's church,
We wait, and see, and search
For answers or help from the Book or tradition,
Ignoring how reason impowers our mission:
Go, light the lamp, and march!

Words: Georg Retzlaff (b. 1946)
Music: *Es ist ein Schnitter*, Regensburg 1638

86 12 12 6

Sunday closest to November 16

Proper 28

Matthew 25:14-30

Jesus said, "For it is as if a man, going on a journey, summoned his slaves and entrusted his property to them; to one he gave five talents, to another two, to another one, to each according to his ability. Then he went away. The one who had received the five talents went off at once and traded with them, and made five more talents. In the same way, the one who had the two talents made two more talents. But the one who had received the one talent went off and dug a hole in the ground and hid his master's money. After a long time the master of those slaves came and settled accounts with them. Then the one who had received the five talents came forward, bringing five more talents, saying, 'Master, you handed over to me five talents; see, I have made five more talents.' His master said to him, 'Well done, good and trustworthy slave; you have been trustworthy in a few things, I will put you in charge of many things; enter into the joy of your master.' And the one with the two talents also came forward, saying, 'Master, you handed over to me two talents; see, I have made two more talents.' His master said to him, 'Well done, good and trustworthy slave; you have been trustworthy in a few things, I will put you in charge of many things; enter into the joy of your master.' Then the one who had received the one talent also came forward, saying, 'Master, I knew that you were a harsh man, reaping where you did not sow, and gathering where you did not scatter seed; so I was afraid, and I went and hid your talent in the ground. Here you have what is yours.' But his master replied, 'You wicked and lazy slave! You knew, did you, that I reap where I did not sow, and gather where I did not scatter? Then you ought to have invested my money with the bankers, and on my return I would have received what was my own with interest. So take the talent from him, and give it to the one with the ten talents. For to all those who have, more will be given, and they will have an abundance; but from those who have nothing, even what they have will be taken away. As for this worthless slave, throw him into the outer darkness, where there will be weeping and gnashing of teeth.'

What treasures, riches, talents He,
Our God has giv'n, entrusted,
To us, His servants, so that we
Would grow in us His Kingdom!
But out of fear,
Or laziness,
We hide our true conviction,
Reject His benediction.

Accept today our pledge, o Lord,
That we shall strive to follow,
The pattern of those who explored
A deeper faith commitment,
Who wagered, gave,
Invested, hoped
For life in all its newness:
A people bold and fearless.

Words: Georg Retzlaff (b. 1946)
Music: *Was Gott tut das ist wohlgetan*, Severus Gastorius, 1675

87 87 44 77

Last Sunday after Pentecost

Christ the King

Matthew 25:31-46

Jesus said, "When the Son of Man comes in his glory, and all the angels with him, then he will sit on the throne of his glory. All the nations will be gathered before him, and he will separate people one from another as a shepherd separates the sheep from the goats, and he will put the sheep at his right hand and the goats at the left. Then the king will say to those at his right hand, 'Come, you that are blessed by my Father, inherit the kingdom prepared for you from the foundation of the world; for I was hungry and you gave me food, I was thirsty and you gave me something to drink, I was a stranger and you welcomed me, I was naked and you gave me clothing, I was sick and you took care of me, I was in prison and you visited me.' Then the righteous will answer him, 'Lord, when was it that we saw you hungry and gave you food, or thirsty and gave you something to drink? And when was it that we saw you a stranger and welcomed you, or naked and gave you clothing? And when was it that we saw you sick or in prison and visited you?' And the king will answer them, 'Truly I tell you, just as you did it to one of the least of these who are members of my family, you did it to me.' Then he will say to those at his left hand, 'You that are accursed, depart from me into the eternal fire prepared for the devil and his angels; for I was hungry and you gave me no food, I was thirsty and you gave me nothing to drink, I was a stranger and you did not welcome me, naked and you did not give me clothing, sick and in prison and you did not visit me.' Then they also will answer, 'Lord, when was it that we saw you hungry or thirsty or a stranger or naked or sick or in prison, and did not take care of you?' Then he will answer them, 'Truly I tell you, just as you did not do it to one of the least of these, you did not do it to me.' And these will go away into eternal punishment, but the righteous into eternal life."

God's judgment is now, today He is speaking:
If you desire life, are earnestly seeking
Eternal compassion and earthly redemption,
Then be and bear fruit, give glory to the King!

If good you would do, you will not remember,
No rules can ever guide your actions, the Tempter,
Though, will you inspire reward to require,
Resist and bear fruit, give glory to the King!

Those who would see God as sheep on His right hand,
Forgo all human pride, and still on His side stand,
O'erwhelmed with thanksgiving for being the living,
Who heard and bore fruit, gave glory to the King.

Words: Georg Retzlaff (b. 1946)
Music: *Die Gedanken sind frei*, Swiss Folk tune, c. 1800

11 11 11 11

Feast of the Presentation

Luke 2:22-40

When the time came for their purification according to the law of Moses, the parents of Jesus brought him up to Jerusalem to present him to the Lord (as it is written in the law of the Lord, "Every firstborn male shall be designated as holy to the Lord"), and they offered a sacrifice according to what is stated in the law of the Lord, "a pair of turtledoves or two young pigeons." Now there was a man in Jerusalem whose name was Simeon; this man was righteous and devout, looking forward to the consolation of Israel, and the Holy Spirit rested on him. It had been revealed to him by the Holy Spirit that he would not see death before he had seen the Lord's Messiah. Guided by the Spirit, Simeon came into the temple; and when the parents brought in the child Jesus, to do for him what was customary under the law, Simeon took him in his arms and praised God, saying,"Master, now you are dismissing your servant in peace, according to your word; for my eyes have seen your salvation, which you have prepared in the presence of all peoples, a light for revelation to the Gentiles and for glory to your people Israel." And the child's father and mother were amazed at what was being said about him. Then Simeon blessed them and said to his mother Mary, "This child is destined for the falling and the rising of many in Israel, and to be a sign that will be opposed so that the inner thoughts of many will be revealed-- and a sword will pierce your own soul too."There was also a prophet, Anna the daughter of Phanuel, of the tribe of Asher. She was of a great age, having lived with her husband seven years after her marriage, then as a widow to the age of eighty-four. She never left the temple but worshiped there with fasting and prayer night and day. At that moment she came, and began to praise God and to speak about the child to all who were looking for the redemption of Jerusalem.When they had finished everything required by the law of the Lord, they returned to Galilee, to their own town of Nazareth. The child grew and became strong, filled with wisdom; and the favor of God was upon him.

Christ, mighty Savior,

Light of all creation,
you make the daytime
radiant with the sunlight
and to our lives give
glittering adornment,
blessings from heaven.

Now comes the morning
as the sun is rising;
splendor of daybreak,
pledge of resurrection;
while in the heavens
angel choirs appearing
join in our worship.

Therefore we come now
kneeling here before you,
joyfully chanting holy
hymns to praise you,
with all creation
joining hearts and voices
singing your glory.

Give heed, we pray you,
to our supplication;
that you may grant us
pardon for offenses,
strength for our weak hearts,
willingness to serve you,
now and for ever.

Into your Temple,
as the infant Jesus,
we come now praying
that you may receive us
and our Selves to
be a worthy off'ring
to your Holy Name.

Words: Georg Retzlaff (b. 1946)
Tune: Mighty Savior, David Hurd, (b. 1950)
HPEC 1982, 35

56 56 56 5

All Saints' Day

Matthew 5:1-12

When Jesus saw the crowds, he went up the mountain; and after he sat down, his disciples came to him. Then he began to speak, and taught them, saying: "Blessed are the poor in spirit, for theirs is the kingdom of heaven. "Blessed are those who mourn, for they will be comforted. "Blessed are the meek, for they will inherit the earth. "Blessed are those who hunger and thirst for righteousness, for they will be filled. "Blessed are the merciful, for they will receive mercy. "Blessed are the pure in heart, for they will see God. "Blessed are the peacemakers, for they will be called children of God. "Blessed are those who are persecuted for righteousness' sake, for theirs is the kingdom of heaven. "Blessed are you when people revile you and persecute you and utter all kinds of evil against you falsely on my account. Rejoice and be glad, for your reward is great in heaven, for in the same way they persecuted the prophets who were before you.

Throughout all times and ages
our God has called our race
to change our ways of error
and new paths to embrace.

We thank Thee, God Almighty,
That many heard Thy call,
And followed in Thy footsteps,
Gave life and goods and all.

We raise our feeble voices
To worship Thee on high;
We know not how to praise Thee
but for Thy Spirit nigh.
With angels and archangels
And all the host of heaven
We join celestial choirs
Of all those who entered life.

All praise be to the Father
and to our Lord, the Son.
Who, through the Spirit's power,
Have us salvation won.
When we, lost in our nature,
Were deaf to hope and faith,
God opened up our ears to
Hear: Be ye now my Saints.

Words: Georg Retzlaff (b. 1946)
Music: *Het Wilhelmus*, Adriaen Valerius, 1626
76 76 D

All Souls' Day

John 14:1-14

Jesus said, "Do not let your hearts be troubled. Believe in God, believe also in me. In my Father's house there are many dwelling places. If it were not so, would I have told you that I go to prepare a place for you? And if I go and prepare a place for you, I will come again and will take you to myself, so that where I am, there you may be also. And you know the way to the place where I am going." Thomas said to him, "Lord, we do not know where you are going. How can we know the way?" Jesus said to him, "I am the way, and the truth, and the life. No one comes to the Father except through me. If you know me, you will know my Father also. From now on you do know him and have seen him." Philip said to him, "Lord, show us the Father, and we will be satisfied." Jesus said to him, "Have I been with you all this time, Philip, and you still do not know me? Whoever has seen me has seen the Father. How can you say, `Show us the Father'? Do you not believe that I am in the Father and the Father is in me? The words that I say to you I do not speak on my own; but the Father who dwells in me does his works. Believe me that I am in the Father and the Father is in me; but if you do not, then believe me because of the works themselves. Very truly, I tell you, the one who believes in me will also do the works that I do and, in fact, will do greater works than these, because I am going to the Father. I will do whatever you ask in my name, so that the Father may be glorified in the Son. If in my name you ask me for anything, I will do it."

He is the Way, the Truth, the Life,
On ev'ry path of joy or strife.
Right here and now Christ is the Way,
To guide us to His Kingdom's day.
Ring out our praise, o bell be heard,
Christ Jesus is the Living Word.

With truth and light Spring breezes play
To melt our Winter hearts away.
Let ev'ry bud and branch and tree
Join young and old in sympathy.
Ring out our praise, o bell, be heard,
Christ Jesus is the Living Word.

We die to self to welcome space
For new life in His Summer's Grace.
As Autumn days approach us fast,
We hope to bear the fruits that last.
Ring out our praise, o bell, be heard,
Christ Jesus is the Living Word.

Words: Joy L. Retzlaff (b. 1939)
Music: *Melita*, John Bacchus Dykes (1823-1876)
HPEC 1982, 579

88 88 88

Appendix

All German folk tunes can be looked up and listened to at www.notendownload. com. YouTube and the Cyberhymnal provide good sources for listening to those melodies for which new lyrics have been written. Below is a small selection which may be helpful in determining the usefulness of a hymn in question.

Gospel texts for Lectionary Year A are from the New Revised Standard Version of the Bible, copyright © 1989 National Council of the Churches of Christ in the USA. Used by permission. All rights reserved.

Epiphany VII	http://hymntime.com/tch/htm/l/b/t/lbtwmrul.htm
Ash Wednesday	http://www.youtube.com/watch?v=JIJ3jkQ3JkU
Lent II	http://www.youtube.com/watch?v=_lCld9uV2yM
Lent III	http://nethymnal.org/htm/i/i/iigowise.htm
Lent IV	http://cyberhymnal.org/htm/i/n/h/inhourmd.htm
Lent V	http://www.youtube.com/watch?v=GxPzikrr75Q&feature=r elated
Palm Sunday	http://smallchurchmusic.com/MP3-2010/MP3- GodWhoseName-Haslemere-PipeLC-128-CAM.mp3
Maundy Thursday	http://www.allmusic.com/performance/christ-mighty-savior- mighty-savior-f1054658
Good Friday	http://nethymnal.org/htm/l/e/letalltw.htm
Ascension Day	http://www.youtube.com/watch?v=tA- Do7WPaQO&feature=related
Easter VII	http://www.youtube.com/watch?v=RUhGlU00tHs&feature= related
Pentecost	http://www.youtube.com/watch?v=gRxbaOPOa-A
Trinity	http://www.youtube.com/watch?=RUhGlU00tHs&feature=r elated
Proper 1	http://www.smallchurchmusic.com/Snippet-2010/S- ForThoseWeLove-Gaza-PipeSKL-48-CAM.mp3
Proper 3	http://hymntime.com/tch/htm/o/b/r/obrighti.htm

Proper 4	http://www.hymnprint.net/index.cfm?go=cCatalog.showCatalogByTune&search=M&tune=14
Proper 5	http://www.youtube.com/watch?v=OOSr6qp-ELk
Proper 6	http://www.youtube.com/watch?v=YzWjEaN8vrw
Proper 13	http://www.youtube.com/watch?v=JmDRb6ZR1Kk
All Saints'	http://www.youtube.com/watch?v=jqKofbyWv1A&feature=related